Consumption Tax Trends

VAT/GST AND EXCISE RATES, TRENDS AND ADMINISTRATION ISSUES

2004 Edition

OECD

ORGANISATION FOR ECONOMIC CO-OPERATION AND DEVELOPMENT

ORGANISATION FOR ECONOMIC CO-OPERATION AND DEVELOPMENT

The OECD is a unique forum where the governments of 30 democracies work together to address the economic, social and environmental challenges of globalisation. The OECD is also at the forefront of efforts to understand and to help governments respond to new developments and concerns, such as corporate governance, the information economy and the challenges of an ageing population. The Organisation provides a setting where governments can compare policy experiences, seek answers to common problems, identify good practice and work to co-ordinate domestic and international policies.

The OECD member countries are: Australia, Austria, Belgium, Canada, the Czech Republic, Denmark, Finland, France, Germany, Greece, Hungary, Iceland, Ireland, Italy, Japan, Korea, Luxembourg, Mexico, the Netherlands, New Zealand, Norway, Poland, Portugal, the Slovak Republic, Spain, Sweden, Switzerland, Turkey, the United Kingdom and the United States. The Commission of the European Communities takes part in the work of the OECD.

OECD Publishing disseminates widely the results of the Organisation's statistics gathering and research on economic, social and environmental issues, as well as the conventions, guidelines and standards agreed by its members.

This work is published on the responsibility of the Secretary-General of the OECD. The opinions expressed and arguments employed herein do not necessarily reflect the official views of the Organisation or of the governments of its member countries.

Also available in French under the title:

Tendances des impôts sur la consommation

TVA/TPS et droits d'accise : taux, tendances et questions d'administration

Foreword

This publication is the fifth in the series "Consumption Tax Trends". It presents information relative to indirect taxes in OECD member countries, as at 1 January 2003.

As in the earlier editions of Consumption Tax Trends, *this edition illustrates the increasing importance of general consumption taxes as revenue instruments in OECD member countries. It also highlights the features underlying this development. In addition, it identifies the large number of differences which exist in respect to the consumption tax base, rates and implementation rules between tax administrations.*

This edition's special features highlight specific aspects of developments in international issues on taxation of services and intangibles and on emerging approaches for financial services. It also deals with tax administration issues.

Table of Contents

Introduction 7

Chapter 1. **Taxing Consumption** 9

Chapter 2. **Consumption Tax Topics** 15

Chapter 3. **Value Added Tax/Tax on Goods and Services Yield, Rates and Structures** 19

Chapter 4. **Selected Excise Duties in OECD Member Countries** 43

Chapter 5. **Taxing Vehicles** 59

Chapter 6. **Globalisation of Services and Intangibles: the Consumption Tax Challenge** 65

Chapter 7. **Financial Services – Emerging Approaches to a Perennial Problem** 69

Chapter 8. **Reducing VAT Revenue Leakage: Improved Approaches are Needed in Many Countries** 75

Annex 1. **Table of exchange rates** 79

Annex 2. **Guidelines on E-commerce and Consumption Tax Guidance Series** 80

Annex 3. **Environmentally related taxes** 106

List of Figures

1.1. Average tax revenue as a percentage of aggregate taxation, by category of tax 10
3.1. Standard rate of VAT at 1 January, 2003 34
4.1. Excise duties per litre of alc./vol. 46

List of Tables

3.1. Taxes on general consumption (5110) as percentage of GDP 21
3.2. Taxes on general consumption (5110) as percentage of total taxation 22
3.3. Taxes on specific goods and services (5120) as percentage of GDP 24
3.4. Taxes on specific goods and services (5120) as percentage of total taxation 25
3.5. VAT/GST rates in OECD member countries 26
3.6. Annual turnover concessions for VAT/GST registration and collection 27
3.7. Departures from standard exemptions 29
3.8. Coverage of different VAT rates 31
3.9. Special VAT taxation methods 35
3.10. Import/export of goods by individuals 37
4.1. Taxation of beer 48

4.2. Taxation of wine 50
4.3. Taxation of alcoholic beverages 52
4.4. Taxation of mineral oils (per 1 000 litres of product at 15° C) 54
4.5. Taxation of tobacco 56
5.1. VAT on sale and registration of motor vehicles 62
5.2. Excise on sale and registration of motor vehicles 63

Introduction

Consumption taxes continue to form an important source of revenue for an increasing number of governments. On average, value added taxes and excise taxes now account for 30% of all revenue collected by governments across the OECD. VAT is now the principal form of taxing consumption whilst excise taxes are raising less revenue. This probably reflects a growing preference for broad-based taxation of the full range of goods and services, as opposed to taxing specific goods. Increasingly excise is used as a means of influencing consumer behaviour, especially with many countries imposing high rates of excise on tobacco goods and on oil products.

Value added tax

Since the publication of the fourth edition of *Consumption Tax Trends* in 2001 there have been a number of developments concerning consumption taxes generally. Further to the developments in electronic commerce the European Union implemented in 2003 its VAT Directive applying a zero-rate for the export of these services and, in the same time, imposing VAT on those electronic services provided to customers in the EU from suppliers outside.

Note also that ten new member states joined the EU on 1st May 2004 and among them four OECD member countries (Czech Republic, Slovak Republic, Hungary and Poland).

In other respects, the continuing globalisation of trade, especially in the services and intangibles area continues to impose pressure on value added tax systems. In this environment, tax authorities need to address the problems of double taxation, lack of clear rules and uncertainty for suppliers. These challenges come in a variety of forms:

- The search to enhance neutrality by reducing the undesirable consequences of exemption from VAT.
- The review of methods for taxing cross-border transactions that involve services and intangibles.
- To improve efficiency of tax administrations and reduce compliance costs for business, minimising the potential for tax evasion and avoidance.

These developments, which are discussed in more detail hereafter, show that OECD revenue authorities are prepared to address the challenges of globalisation in the interests of both business and citizens.

Excise taxes and vehicle taxation

As in previous editions, the latest *Consumption Tax Trends* reports on the excise taxes that the member countries levy on a number of specific products, including alcoholic beverages, mineral oil products and tobacco products. It also provides a detailed survey of vehicle taxes.

Environmentally related taxes

The fourth edition of *Consumption Tax Trends* devoted a long chapter to environmentally related taxes. Although the subject is still a timely one, it is not necessary to publish another chapter on it given that essential information is now available in the recent publication "*OECD Environmental Data Compendium 2004*". The tables on environmentally related taxes are reproduced in Annex 3 to this publication.

This information is taken from the "*OECD Environmental Data Compendium 2004*". The tables on environmentally related taxes may be consulted free of charge at the following address: *www.oecd.org/env/tax-database*.

CONSUMPTION TAX TRENDS – ISBN 92-64-00676-1 – © OECD 2005

ISBN 92-64-00676-1
Consumption Tax Trends
VAT/GST and Excise Rates, Trends and Administration Issues

Chapter 1

Taxing Consumption

Consumption and taxation

In the OECD classification "taxes" are confined to compulsory, unrequited payments to general government. They are shared into five broad categories: income and profits; payroll; property; consumption and compulsory social security contributions, which are treated as taxes (see *Revenue Statistics 1965-2003*).

In common language, consumption taxes (a sub-category of Taxes on Goods and Services) are sometimes called *indirect taxes* in the sense that they do not reach directly profits or income (like *direct* taxes) but transactions (like a service or a transfer of property).

In the statistical nomenclature of the OECD, consumption taxes are split into two categories:

- *General* consumption taxes, *i.e.* essentially Value Added Tax (VAT) and its equivalent, the Goods and Services Tax (GST). This category also includes the "sales tax" collected by state and local authorities in the United States, which is also levied on consumption but differs significantly.
- Taxes on *specific* goods and services, consisting primarily of excise taxes. It also includes customs duties and certain special taxes on insurance or financial operations, which are not covered in *Consumption Tax Trends*.

Looking at the unweighted average of revenue from both these categories of taxes as a percentage of overall taxation in the OECD member countries (see Tables 3.2 and 3.4 below), it can be seen that the proportion is roughly 30%. In 2002, this broke down to one-third for taxes on specific goods and services and two-thirds for general consumption taxes.

Figure 1.1. **Average tax revenue as a percentage of aggregate taxation, by category of tax**

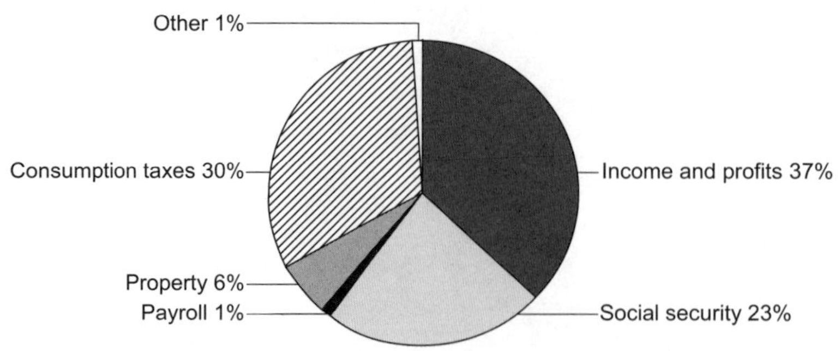

Source: OECD Revenue Statistics 1965-2003.

General consumption taxes

Value Added Tax (VAT) is becoming one of the most widespread consumption tax collection mechanisms in the world. Since July 2000 and Australia's successful adoption of

Goods and Services Tax (GST-equivalent to VAT), 29 of the Organisation's 30 member countries now operate VAT. Only the United States, for historical and constitutional reasons, has retained a sales tax system in which all of the tax is collected at the final stage of consumption. In addition, as of 1 May, 2004, when ten new member States joined the European Union, 19 of the 30 OECD member countries now share a common system based on the EU's 6th VAT Directive. It is for this reason that some countries' data refer to the system applicable as from 1 May 2004, even though most of them show data in effect at 1 January 2003.

General functioning

Whichever name is assigned to it – VAT or GST – the system is based on tax collection in a staged process, with successive taxpayers entitled to deduct input tax on purchases and account for output tax on sales. Each business in the supply chain takes part in the process of controlling and collecting the tax, remitting the proportion of tax corresponding to the margin realised on each transaction, or the difference between the VAT paid out to suppliers and the VAT charged to customers. In practice, all OECD countries with value-added taxes impose the tax at all stages and normally allow immediate deduction of taxes on purchases by all but the final consumer.

In international trade in tangible goods, system continuity is ensured by the filtering role of the customs system. Exported goods are subject to a zero rate (and are cleansed of any residual VAT via successive taxpayers' deductions of input tax), whilst imports are subject to the same VAT as equivalent domestic goods. This VAT on imports is generally collected at the same time as customs duties, although in some countries this collection is postponed until declared on the importer's next VAT return. Deduction of the VAT incurred at importation, in the same way as input tax deduction on a domestic supply, ensures neutrality and no distortion of international trade.

Within the European Union, which abolished internal customs barriers and tax frontiers in 1993, the system of intra-Community delivery (exempt in the goods' country of origin) and intra-Community acquisition (taxed in the country of destination) that performs the filtering role that operates in normal imports/export regimes.

The nature of services and intangible products means that mechanisms other than those used for tangible goods must be found. In the days when technical capabilities limited remote provision of services, a number of mechanisms were used to achieve neutrality. Within the European Union, the 6th VAT Directive of 1977 (77/399/EEC) – which is still in force today – stipulates a basic rule that services should be taxed where the supplier is established (an origin rule). However, recognising that this would breach neutrality in many cases, there are a large number of exceptions to this basic rule. Most tangible services are taxed in the country in which they are in fact performed (*e.g.* car hire, construction work, passenger transport, etc.), whereas intangible services (*e.g.* intellectual services, consulting, etc.) are taxed in the country in which the business customer is located. For countries outside the EU, the place in which such services and digital products are taxed is determined according to where they are effectively consumed.

The rapid growth of international services and intangible products between business enterprises, and subsequently the delivery of such products to individuals thanks to technology has changed this profoundly. Governments understood that it was vital to react collectively to this new challenge. The first manifestation of this determination was reflected in the principles welcomed by Ministers in Ottawa in October 1998.

Electronic commerce

At the Ottawa Conference, framework conditions for the taxation of electronic commerce were established.

Framework conditions for consumption tax on electronic commerce

- Rules for the consumption taxation of cross-border trade should result in taxation in the jurisdiction where consumption takes place.
- For the purpose of consumption taxes, the supply of digitised products should not be treated as a supply of goods.
- Where business and other organisations within a country acquire services and intangible property from suppliers outside the country, countries should examine the use of reverse charge, self-assessment or other equivalent mechanisms where this would give immediate protection of their revenue base and of the competitiveness of domestic suppliers.

In 2001, after two years' work in co-operation with businesses and a number of non-member countries, the OECD's Committee on Fiscal Affairs (CFA) adopted guidelines for determining the place of consumption in respect of cross-border delivery of services and digital property:

- For business-to-business transactions, it is the jurisdiction in which the recipient has established its business presence.
- For business-to-consumer transactions, it is the jurisdiction in which the recipient has his or her usual place of residence.

For business-to-business supplies adoption of the reverse charge is recommended as the means of ensuring collection, whereas for business-to-consumer transactions, the report signals the possibility of harnessing new technologies in the medium-term while acknowledging that simplified, registration-based mechanisms may prove necessary in the interim.

In addition, the 2001 report recognised that further work was needed for full development of the Ottawa taxation framework conditions. From a business standpoint, it is vital that VAT/GST be applied properly at the time a transaction takes place, since it is rarely possible to correct errors after the fact in an environment characterised by a minimum of human intervention, especially in the business-to-consumer sector of electronic commerce.

Accordingly, the CFA decided to formulate a series of consumption tax guidance papers for tax administrations. Among those currently available, those dealing with verification of the customer's status and tax collection jurisdiction are especially useful in the application of VAT to electronic commerce transactions. This Guidance is annexed to this publication. Initially geared to electronic commerce issues, they are to be expanded to cover a wider range of issues involving consumption taxes.

The CFA also approved in 2003 a Report on the Committee's work to-date. The full documentation is available on the Internet site of the OECD Centre for Tax Policy and Administration (*www.oecd.org/ctp*).

Latest developments

The current edition of *Consumption Tax Trends* reports on the state of OECD work in this field, focusing more specifically on:

- A review of the application of VAT to the cross-border trade in services or intangible products, so as to avert double taxation or unintentional non-taxation, and to lessen the obstacles to the development of global trade.
- Ways to enhance neutrality by reducing the unwanted consequences of VAT/GST exemption in certain industries, including the financial services sector.
- Improving the efficiency of tax administrations, reducing the cost of tax compliance for taxpayers, and the fight against tax evasion and avoidance.
- Bolstering international co-operation between tax authorities.

The latest developments in the field of tax policy at the OECD can be monitored on the Web site of the Centre for Tax Policy and Administration, at the following address: *www.oecd.org/ctp*.

In addition, selected tables from the biennial publication *Consumption Tax Trends* are updated annually in the OECD tax database and may be consulted at the following address: *www.oecd.org/ctp/taxdatabase*.

Taxes on specific goods and services: excise taxes

A number of general characteristics differentiate excise duties from value added taxes:

- they are levied on a limited range of products;
- they are not normally liable until the goods are entered into free circulation, often at a late stage in the supply chain;
- excise charges are generally assessed by reference to the weight, volume, strength or quantity of the product, combined in some cases, with *ad valorem* taxes.

Consequently, as opposed to VAT, the excise system is characterised by a small number of taxpayers in several domains at the manufacturing, distributive or wholesale stage.

Originally aimed at raising revenues, excise taxes may cover a very wide range of products like salt, sugar, matches, fruit juice or chocolates. However, the range of products subject to excise taxes has declined with the expansion of general consumption taxes. Excise taxes on alcohol, tobacco and hydrocarbon oils continue to raise significant revenues to governments.

Excise taxes covered in *Consumption Tax Trends* are those levied in most member countries on tobacco goods, alcoholic drinks and hydrocarbon oils. There has been a discernible trend in recent years to ascribe to these taxes characteristics other than simply revenue rising. They are increasingly referred to in terms of taxes to influence consumer behaviour, such as reducing environmentally harmful emissions from cars and other means of transport, and encouraging reductions in consumption of tobacco and alcohol products for health reasons.

ISBN 92-64-00676-1
Consumption Tax Trends
VAT/GST and Excise Rates, Trends and Administration Issues

Chapter 2

Consumption Tax Topics

Value added taxes

The Value Added Tax (VAT or GST) system has for many years demonstrated its capacity to raise tax revenue in a neutral and transparent manner, and more and more countries around the world are adopting this method of taxation. Following the successful introduction of GST in Australia from 1st July 2000, the United States is now the only OECD member country without a value added tax. The US continues to deploy retail sales taxes at the State level (and below), rather than a federal consumption tax. These taxes are not without their own problems, especially now that electronic commerce has made purchasing goods across state borders without addition of tax even easier than it was before. With a Supreme Court ruling making it difficult for states to require tax collection on all cross-border sales there are increasing pressures on state legislators from "bricks and mortar" retailers to level this particular playing field.

The development of VAT in the context of globalisation, technical and commercial changes and governments' increasing concerns about tax evasion, make adaptation necessary. Without altering the principles involved, the task is to keep the rules fair for businesses and enable tax authorities to be more effective at ensuring compliance with those rules and promoting service to taxpayers. This trend entails heightened co-operation between tax authorities and a more strategic approach to the management of these issues.

The fourth edition of *Consumption Tax Trends* highlighted one particular aspect of the challenges that globalisation poses for the collection of general consumption taxes: electronic commerce. In this connection, tax authorities have become aware of the need to take a system that is based on national tax boundaries and adapt it to the borderless world of global trade.

In 2003 the European Union implemented its VAT Directive requiring the collection of VAT in the member State of consumption on a range of electronic services provided by suppliers outside the EU to consumers inside. Under the Directive a non-EU supplier is required to charge and collect VAT from customers in the EU. To help in this the supplier may take advantage of a special scheme under which all contacts are with one member State only, rather than having to deal with, potentially, 25 countries. The member State of registration collects the VAT due and subsequently distributes it to the member States in accordance with the declaration made by the supplier. More importantly from an EU perspective, was the change made, in the same Directive, under which exports of electronic services to customers outside the EU are now treated as exports and are, effectively, zero-rated. The EU is committed to a review of the Directive by 2006.

The challenge is not limited to electronic commerce, however, and globalisation of trade continues to bring pressure on the international aspects of value added taxes. The treatment of goods is generally less problematic, although even here global contracting can mean supplies of goods being made in a domestic market by a supplier with no presence in the jurisdiction. The problems with services and intangibles are greater and a recent report by the OECD illustrated the extent to which these are causing problems of double taxation, lack of clear rules and uncertainty for suppliers (*The Application of Consumption Taxes to the International Trade in Services and Intangibles*, July 2004 *www.oecd.org/ctp*). The OECD will be examining these problems over the next couple of years with a view to making recommendations on how best to resolve them. This topic is explored in greater detail in Chapter VI.

The problems caused by exemption from VAT continue. Exemption frequently leads to a lack of neutrality because of the inherent inability to recover input tax incurred in connection with exempt outputs. The financial services sector is probably the most affected by this so it was with considerable interest to tax legislators and commentators that New Zealand changed its rules on financial services quite radically in 2003. As will be seen in Chapter VII New Zealand now applies a comparatively wide zero rate to financial services, although it should be noted that at the same time they introduced, for the first time, a reverse charge on imported services. It is questionable as to how far other countries will follow this approach given that the revenue implications of such a move would prove very expensive, especially for those with major financial service sectors. Financial service issues have been further illustrated by the European Commission's decision to undertake a review of the current legislation governing financial services. The review is likely, however, to be limited to updating the rules to reflect the major changes in the sector in recent years, rather than a fundamental overhaul of exemption.

Despite the growth in popularity of VAT amongst governments, there has been a significant and worrying trend in recent years for the tax to become a target for serious criminal activity. Carousel frauds within the EU mushroomed in the late 1990s and into the 21st century. These frauds take advantage of the rules for intra-Community trade in goods that allow for an effective zero-rate on a sale from one member State to another. Similar types of serious fraud have occurred in Canada, especially with trade in used cars. The amounts of tax involved in all these serious frauds have become a cause for significant concern for both finance ministers and tax administrators. Responses have been administrative, through increased resources being targeted to interdiction of fraud activity and, in some cases, legislative. The UK has, through a very open process, conducted a review of indirect tax losses (excise, as well as VAT) and, as a result, has developed an overall strategy to counter all types of losses rather than those lost through specific frauds. Part of that strategy has been new legislation imposing joint and several liability on all businesses within the supply chain for goods commonly involved in carousel frauds. Germany and the Netherlands have also introduced similar legislation. Whilst it is too early to report how successful these measures have been, early indications are that they are having a positive impact. This topic is explored in greater detail in Chapter VIII.

Developments in information technology have meant that governments across the OECD countries have sought ways to improve services to taxpayers. Given the regular contact businesses have with tax authorities it is not surprising that many countries have introduced on-line registration and reporting facilities for VAT. Italy, for example, now requires all VAT returns to be rendered electronically, either directly or through an intermediary. Overall, the progressive use of technology should lead to reduced compliance costs for business and better use of resources for tax administrations.

More than ever, the OECD's Committee on Fiscal Affairs and its Working Party on Consumption Taxes are the forums in which the major players in this area can join forces to establish basic principles that can guide government in implementing a more harmonious tax system, without infringing national sovereignty.

Excise taxes

After a lengthy decline, specific consumption taxes stabilised in recent years as a proportion of aggregate taxation (Table 3.4 below). Apart from their role as a source of tax revenue, excise taxes have confirmed over time that they also fulfil social and environmental functions, since changes in the rates and structure of excise tax have affected consumer behaviour in certain areas. Even so, while they share similar objectives, excise tax rates and bases still vary widely from one OECD country to another, something that influences cross-border shopping and can often have a significant impact on certain businesses located in border areas.

ISBN 92-64-00676-1
Consumption Tax Trends
VAT/GST and Excise Rates, Trends and Administration Issues

Chapter 3

Value Added Tax
Tax on Goods and Services
Yield, Rates and Structures

Introduction

Although the majority of countries have adopted a general consumption tax system (called VAT or GST) based on multi-stage payment and the entitlement to deduct input taxes, there remain many differences in the way it is implemented, including between OECD member countries, because of the continued existence of lower rates, exemptions and special arrangements to meet specific policy objectives. These differences remain, even between EU member States whose VAT laws share the same legislative root, namely the 6th VAT Directive.

These differences, for the most part, run counter to the philosophy of VAT which was designed initially to be more coherent in structure and simpler to administer and collect. Yet despite globalisation and the expansion of world trade, countries' continuing tax sovereignty remains essential. In the present circumstances, a harmonised system applied in all countries is out of the question. This does not, however, mean that there are not a number of shared basic principles which guarantee a measure of consistency amidst the diversity, preventing double taxation, involuntary non-taxation and distortion of competition.

Furthermore, the pressure that globalisation exerts on governments and tax authorities is increasing their determination to remedy the discrepancies liable to generate distortions of competition or give rise to tax evasion, to reduce the cost of compliance with tax obligations and to implement the necessary simplifications.

Importance of and trend in consumption taxes

Taxes on general consumption

Tables 3.1 and 3.2 show that, following a period during which it gradually increased, the revenue from taxes on general consumption, mainly in the form of VAT receipts, stabilised after 2000 as a percentage of both GDP and total taxation. This average stability also reflects great stability in the OECD countries as a whole. Australia (which adopted VAT in 2000), South Korea, Luxemburg and New Zealand are the only countries to have seen taxes on general consumption increase in relation to GDP – by at least 0.5 percentage points, while in Hungary and Iceland the percentage has fallen between 2000 and 2002 in the same proportion (by 0.9 and 1.2 points, respectively).

It is apparent that, over the longer term, the OECD member countries have relied increasingly on taxes on general consumption to provide their tax revenue. Since 1965, the share of taxes on general consumption as a percentage of GDP has almost doubled as an unweighted average, rising from 3.8% to 6.8%. The share has also risen by a third compared with total taxation (up from 13.5% to 18.7%).

This is especially true of VAT, which has been introduced in all but one of the OECD countries. Following the recent introduction of the GST in Australia, the United States is the only OECD country not to have adopted a VAT-type consumption tax. Greece, Spain and

 CONSUMPTION TAX TRENDS – ISBN 92-64-00676-1 – © OECD 2005

Table 3.1. **Taxes on general consumption (5110) as percentage of GDP***

	1965	1970	1975	1980	1985	1990	1995	2000	2001	2002
Canada	4.6	4.4	4.0	3.6	4.3	5.1	5.0	5.1	5.2	5.2
Mexico				2.5	2.7	3.6	2.8	3.5	3.6	3.5
United States	1.2	1.6	1.8	1.9	2.0	2.2	2.2	2.3	2.2	2.2
Australia	1.6	1.6	1.8	1.4	2.3	2.4	2.6	3.8	3.9	4.3
Japan	–	–	–	–	–	1.3	1.4	2.4	2.4	2.5
Korea			1.8	3.7	3.4	3.7	3.7	4.0	4.2	4.6
New Zealand	1.8	2.1	2.6	3.1	3.2	8.5	8.4	8.3	8.6	8.8
Austria	6.3	6.4	7.4	8.0	8.8	8.4	7.6	8.2	8.1	8.2
Belgium	6.6	7.4	6.6	7.2	7.2	7.1	6.9	7.4	7.1	7.3
Czech Republic							6.6	7.1	6.9	6.8
Denmark	2.7	7.4	6.8	9.8	9.5	9.8	9.5	9.7	9.7	9.7
Finland	5.6	6.2	5.8	6.3	7.4	8.5	8.0	8.4	8.2	8.4
France[1]	8.0	8.7	8.4	8.6	8.7	8.1	7.6	7.6	7.4	7.3
Germany	5.2	5.5	5.2	6.2	5.9	5.9	6.7	6.9	6.7	6.5
Greece	2.0	3.8	4.0	3.2	4.9	7.8	7.4	8.3	8.6	8.4
Hungary[2]							8.2	10.2	9.9	9.3
Iceland	4.4	6.0	8.5	8.5	9.4	10.2	10.1	11.7	10.4	10.5
Ireland	1.4	3.8	4.3	4.6	7.2	6.9	7.0	7.4	7.0	7.1
Italy	3.3	3.4	3.7	4.8	5.0	5.7	5.7	6.6	6.4	6.4
Luxembourg	3.4	2.8	4.5	4.7	5.8	5.6	5.9	6.0	6.2	6.5
Netherlands	4.1	5.2	5.9	6.9	6.9	7.1	6.5	7.2	7.6	7.5
Norway	6.4	8.2	8.0	7.7	7.8	7.8	8.7	8.3	8.3	8.4
Poland							6.3	7.1	7.0	7.4
Portugal[2]	–	1.6	2.3	3.9	3.3	5.7	7.5	8.4	8.2	
Slovak Republic[2]								7.6	7.3	7.5
Spain	3.3	3.3	2.9	2.3	4.1	5.3	5.2	6.2	6.0	5.9
Sweden	3.6	4.0	5.0	6.3	6.7	7.9	9.4	9.1	9.1	9.2
Switzerland	1.9	1.7	2.1	2.6	2.8	3.0	3.3	4.0	4.0	3.9
Turkey	–	–	–	–	3.6	4.0	7.0	7.8	8.1	8.1
United Kingdom	1.8	2.5	3.1	5.2	6.0	6.0	6.7	6.8	6.8	6.9
Unweighted average:										
OECD total	3.8	4.4	4.6	5.1	5.6	6.1	6.3	6.9	6.8	6.8
OECD America	2.9	3.0	2.9	2.7	3.0	3.6	3.3	3.6	3.7	3.6
OECD Pacific	1.7	1.9	2.1	2.7	3.0	3.9	4.0	4.6	4.8	5.0
OECD Europe	4.1	4.9	5.3	5.9	6.4	6.9	7.2	7.7	7.6	7.6
EU19	4.1	4.8	5.1	5.9	6.5	7.1	7.2	7.7	7.6	7.6
EU15	4.1	4.8	5.1	5.9	6.5	7.1	7.2	7.6	7.5	7.5

* These tables are taken from *Revenue Statistics* which are published annually by the OECD and are based on a nomenclature common to the OECD countries. Category 5110, which covers general taxes on goods and services, is used for Tables 3.1 and 3.2 and includes VAT/GST, sales taxes and other general taxes on goods and services. Category 5120, *Taxes on specific goods and services*, consists primarily of excise taxes, but also includes certain specific taxes such as customs duties and taxes on insurance and certain financial operations in particular. *Revenue Statistics 1965-2003* is for sale at the OECD's on-line bookshop: *www.oecd.org/bookshop*.

1. The tax revenues have been reduced by the amount of the capital transfer. The capital transfer has been allocated between tax headings in proportion to the reported tax revenues.
2. For the year 2002, provisional data published in the *Revenue Statistics* Edition 2003 are used.

Source: Revenue Statistics 1965-2003, 2004 Edition.

Table 3.2. **Taxes on general consumption (5110) as percentage of total taxation***

	1965	1970	1975	1980	1985	1990	1995	2000	2001	2002
Canada	17.8	14.4	12.5	11.5	13.2	14.1	14.0	14.3	15.0	15.3
Mexico				15.7	15.9	20.8	16.9	18.7	19.1	19.3
United States	4.8	5.8	7.0	7.0	7.9	8.0	8.0	7.6	7.7	8.2
Australia	7.4	7.4	6.7	5.3	7.9	8.0	8.7	12.1	13.0	13.5
Japan	–	–	–	–	–	4.3	5.2	8.9	8.9	9.5
Korea			12.7	22.0	21.1	20.4	18.9	17.0	17.2	18.9
New Zealand	7.7	8.0	9.0	10.2	10.4	22.4	22.7	24.7	25.7	25.3
Austria	18.7	18.5	19.8	20.1	21.0	20.8	18.2	18.8	18.0	18.7
Belgium	21.1	21.2	16.3	17.0	15.8	16.5	15.3	16.3	15.5	15.7
Czech Republic							16.7	18.3	17.8	17.3
Denmark	9.1	18.8	16.9	22.3	20.1	20.7	19.3	19.5	19.4	19.9
Finland	18.5	19.3	15.8	17.4	18.3	19.3	17.4	17.4	17.8	18.2
France[1]	23.3	25.5	23.4	21.1	20.0	18.8	17.3	16.8	16.6	16.7
Germany	16.5	17.1	14.6	16.6	15.8	16.6	17.4	18.4	18.2	18.0
Greece	10.3	16.8	18.3	13.2	17.2	26.5	23.0	21.8	23.4	23.5
Hungary[2]							19.4	26.1	25.4	24.3
Iceland	16.7	22.0	28.6	28.9	33.0	32.4	31.7	29.7	27.3	27.6
Ireland	5.7	13.1	14.7	14.8	20.6	20.6	21.2	23.1	23.1	25.0
Italy	12.9	13.2	14.3	15.6	14.5	14.7	13.8	15.4	14.9	15.0
Luxembourg	12.4	10.6	12.1	11.6	12.8	13.9	14.0	15.0	15.1	15.5
Netherlands	12.4	14.6	14.4	15.8	16.2	16.5	15.6	17.4	19.0	19.2
Norway	21.5	23.8	20.5	18.2	18.2	18.8	21.2	19.2	19.2	19.2
Poland							17.1	22.0	21.8	22.6
Portugal[2]	–	8.4	11.2	16.2	12.6	19.6	22.4	23.2	22.9	
Slovak Republic[2]								22.3	23.0	22.7
Spain	22.2	20.3	15.3	10.2	14.7	16.0	15.9	17.5	17.0	16.6
Sweden	10.4	10.3	12.0	13.4	14.0	14.9	19.4	16.8	17.6	18.4
Switzerland	9.4	7.8	7.8	9.2	10.7	11.6	12.0	13.1	13.4	13.0
Turkey	–	–	–	–	23.3	20.1	31.1	24.2	23.0	26.1
United Kingdom	5.9	6.8	8.9	14.7	15.9	16.6	19.2	18.2	18.4	19.4
Unweighted average:										
OECD total	13.5	14.7	14.5	15.3	16.4	17.4	17.7	18.5	18.5	18.7
OECD America	11.3	10.1	9.7	11.4	12.3	14.3	13.0	13.5	13.9	14.3
OECD Pacific	7.5	7.7	9.5	12.5	13.1	13.8	13.9	15.7	16.2	16.8
OECD Europe	14.5	16.0	15.8	16.5	17.6	18.7	19.0	19.6	19.5	19.7
EU19	14.2	15.6	15.2	16.0	16.6	18.1	17.9	19.2	19.2	19.3
EU15	14.2	15.6	15.2	16.0	16.6	18.1	18.0	18.4	18.5	18.6

* These tables are taken from *Revenue Statistics* which are published annually by the OECD and are based on a nomenclature common to the OECD countries. Category 5110, which covers general taxes on goods and services, is used for Tables 3.1 and 3.2 and includes VAT/GST, sales taxes and other general taxes on goods and services. Category 5120, *Taxes on specific goods and services*, consists primarily of excise taxes, but also includes certain specific taxes such as customs duties and taxes on insurance and certain financial operations in particular. *Revenue Statistics 1965-2003* is for sale at the OECD's on-line bookshop: *www.oecd.org/bookshop.*

1. The tax revenues have been reduced by the amount of the capital transfer. The capital transfer has been allocated between tax headings in proportion to the reported tax revenues.
2. For the year 2002, provisional data published in the *Revenue Statistics* Edition 2003 are used.

Source: Revenue Statistics 1965-2003, 2004 Edition.

Portugal introduced VAT in the 1980s when they joined the European Union, while Iceland, Japan and New Zealand followed suit in the same period and Switzerland followed shortly afterwards. The eastern European economies introduced VAT in their turn in the 1990s, some of them adopting the model introduced by the 6th Directive with their future membership of the European Union in mind. The tendency for VAT rates to rise over the long term also contributed to the growing share of general consumption taxes in the tax mix.

Taxes on specific goods and services

With regard to taxes on specific goods and services, the bulk of which are excise taxes, Tables 3.3 and 3.4 show, in contrast, that revenue from such taxes is continuing to fall slowly as a percentage of GDP, though it has stabilised as a percentage of total tax revenue since 2001.

Overall, for the whole of the OECD area, there has over the long term been an increase in revenue from taxes on general consumption as a proportion of total taxation and GDP and a decline in receipts from taxes on specific goods and services compared with the same aggregates. The main reason for this trend is the substitution of VAT/GTS for other consumption taxes.

Excise taxes are discussed in greater detail in Chapter IV.

Revenue Statistics 1965-2003 is for sale at the OECD's on-line bookshop: *www.oecd.org/bookshop*.

Rate and structure of VAT/GST

Looking at Table 3.5 which shows the rates of VAT applying at 1st January 2003, it can be seen that standard rates have remained generally stable since 2000, the date of the previous edition. France was the only country to reduce its rate – from 20.6% to 19.6% – while four countries raised it (Netherlands, Norway, Portugal and Turkey).

The table shows that there are still major differences between the OECD member countries, with standard rates ranging from 5% (Japan) to 25% (Denmark, Hungary, Sweden). However, the vast majority of member countries (23 out of 29) have standard rates of between 15% and 25%, while the (unweighted) average is 17.8%, *i.e.* very slightly up on 2000. It can also be seen that virtually all member countries have abolished the higher rates (over 25%) which existed ten or so yearsago.

In assessing differences in rates, consideration also needs to be given to the existence of lower rates (including zero rates) and exemptions, which mean that a number of goods and services escape taxation at the standard rate (Tables 3.7 and 3.8).

These exceptions cover three categories of product in all:

- Basic essentials (food, medical and hospital care, culture and sport and, in some countries, devices for the disabled people, or water supplies, for example).
- Certain activities considered traditionally to be utilities (public transport, postal services, public television, social services) and also charitable activities.
- Certain sectors that are exempt from VAT for historical or practical reasons and may be subject to specific taxes (property, insurance, financial services).

The thresholds for VAT exemption or registration (compulsory or voluntary) constitute another form of exemption which this time is based not on the nature of the goods or services, but on the size or nature of the firm (Table 3.6). The levels of these thresholds also

Table 3.3. **Taxes on specific goods and services (5120) as percentage of GDP***

	1965	1970	1975	1980	1985	1990	1995	2000	2001	2002
Canada	4.3	4.1	4.3	4.0	4.2	3.7	3.5	3.0	3.1	3.2
Mexico				5.6	8.2	5.9	6.0	6.2	5.9	5.2
United States	3.7	3.2	2.6	2.2	2.1	1.9	2.1	1.9	1.8	1.8
Australia	4.9	4.5	5.1	6.1	6.0	4.5	4.3	4.5	4.5	4.5
Japan	4.5	4.1	3.1	3.6	3.3	2.2	2.2	2.1	2.1	2.1
Korea			6.8	6.6	6.0	4.8	4.3	4.6	5.1	4.6
New Zealand	4.4	4.5	3.9	3.4	3.7	3.5	3.1	2.5	2.5	2.7
Austria	6.1	6.2	5.2	4.0	4.2	3.6	3.3	3.4	3.3	3.4
Belgium	4.0	4.6	4.0	3.8	3.9	3.8	4.0	3.4	3.3	3.4
Czech Republic							5.2	4.3	4.0	3.9
Denmark	8.7	7.0	5.9	5.9	6.1	5.3	5.7	5.6	5.4	5.6
Finland	7.1	6.3	5.9	6.4	6.1	5.7	5.6	5.2	5.1	5.2
France[1]	4.9	4.0	3.2	3.4	3.8	3.8	4.0	3.7	3.5	3.6
Germany	4.6	4.2	3.8	3.5	3.3	3.3	3.6	3.3	3.5	3.6
Greece	6.7	6.1	5.2	6.1	6.0	4.6	5.3	3.9	3.9	3.7
Hungary[2]							8.8	5.4	5.0	4.8
Iceland	11.8	10.3	10.0	8.7	7.5	5.4	4.5	4.7	3.9	3.7
Ireland	10.8	10.5	8.6	8.9	7.7	6.7	5.7	4.5	3.8	3.7
Italy	6.2	6.0	3.6	3.0	3.1	4.1	4.6	4.2	3.9	3.8
Luxembourg	3.1	2.3	3.0	3.8	5.0	4.3	5.2	5.1	4.7	5.1
Netherlands	4.8	4.1	3.4	3.2	3.1	3.2	3.8	3.7	3.6	3.5
Norway	5.5	6.1	6.3	6.9	7.9	6.4	6.7	5.1	4.8	4.6
Poland							6.5	4.6	4.4	4.6
Portugal[2]	6.6	6.6	5.6	6.6	7.6	6.8	5.7	5.2	5.1	
Slovak Republic[2]								4.6	3.2	3.6
Spain	2.7	2.5	1.6	2.4	3.6	3.5	3.4	3.6	3.4	3.4
Sweden	6.7	6.3	4.5	4.3	5.6	4.9	3.8	3.6	3.6	3.7
Switzerland	3.7	3.7	2.9	2.7	2.4	2.1	2.3	2.4	2.5	2.5
Turkey	5.6	6.1	6.5	4.5	1.9	1.5	1.4	5.3	5.5	5.9
United Kingdom	7.7	7.4	5.2	4.7	5.2	4.6	5.0	4.6	4.4	4.3
Unweighted average:										
OECD total	5.8	5.4	4.8	4.8	4.9	4.2	4.5	4.1	4.0	3.9
OECD America	4.0	3.6	3.5	3.9	4.9	3.8	3.9	3.7	3.6	3.4
OECD Pacific	4.6	4.4	4.7	4.9	4.7	3.7	3.5	3.4	3.6	3.5
OECD Europe	6.2	5.8	5.0	4.9	5.0	4.4	4.7	4.3	4.1	4.1
EU19	6.0	5.6	4.6	4.7	5.0	4.5	5.0	4.3	4.1	4.0
EU15	6.0	5.6	4.6	4.7	5.0	4.5	4.6	4.2	4.0	4.0

* These tables are taken from *Revenue Statistics* which are published annually by the OECD and are based on a nomenclature common to the OECD countries. Category 5110, which covers general taxes on goods and services, is used for Tables 3.1 and 3.2 and includes VAT/GST, sales taxes and other general taxes on goods and services. Category 5120, *Taxes on specific goods and services*, consists primarily of excise taxes, but also includes certain specific taxes such as customs duties and taxes on insurance and certain financial operations in particular. *Revenue Statistics 1965-2003* is for sale at the OECD's on-line bookshop: *www.oecd.org/bookshop*.

1. The tax revenues have been reduced by the amount of the capital transfer. The capital transfer has been allocated between tax headings in proportion to the reported tax revenues.
2. For the year 2002, provisional data published in the *Revenue Statistics* Edition 2003 are used.

Source: Revenue Statistics 1965-2003, 2004 Edition.

Table 3.4. Taxes on specific goods and services (5120) as percentage of total taxation*

	1965	1970	1975	1980	1985	1990	1995	2000	2001	2002
Canada	16.8	13.3	13.6	13.0	13.0	10.3	9.9	8.5	9.0	9.5
Mexico				34.4	48.6	34.0	35.8	33.4	31.4	28.6
United States	15.1	11.7	10.0	8.3	8.4	7.0	7.5	6.3	6.4	6.9
Australia	22.7	20.3	19.1	22.6	20.7	15.3	14.5	14.1	14.8	14.3
Japan	25.0	20.9	15.1	14.1	12.1	7.3	8.0	7.8	7.8	8.2
Korea			47.3	39.5	37.4	26.5	21.9	19.7	21.1	18.8
New Zealand	18.5	17.2	13.8	11.2	11.7	9.2	8.5	7.5	7.5	7.6
Austria	18.0	18.0	14.0	10.1	9.9	9.0	7.9	7.7	7.4	7.6
Belgium	13.0	13.3	9.9	9.0	8.5	8.8	8.9	7.4	7.2	7.3
Czech Republic							13.0	11.0	10.4	10.0
Denmark	29.2	17.9	14.7	13.4	13.0	11.2	11.5	11.2	10.9	11.4
Finland	23.4	19.8	16.1	17.7	15.2	12.9	12.1	10.9	11.0	11.3
France[1]	14.3	11.6	9.0	8.4	8.7	8.7	9.1	8.1	7.9	8.1
Germany	14.6	12.9	10.8	9.3	8.7	9.2	9.5	8.8	9.4	10.1
Greece	33.8	27.4	23.9	25.1	20.9	15.6	16.4	10.1	10.7	10.4
Hungary[2]							20.9	13.8	12.8	12.6
Iceland	45.0	37.9	33.6	29.8	26.5	17.0	14.0	11.9	10.3	9.6
Ireland	43.4	36.4	29.7	28.3	22.0	20.1	17.5	13.9	12.6	12.9
Italy	24.1	23.2	14.0	9.7	9.1	10.6	11.1	9.7	9.1	9.0
Luxembourg	11.1	8.7	8.0	9.3	11.1	10.4	12.2	12.6	11.4	12.1
Netherlands	14.7	11.6	8.1	7.3	7.2	7.5	9.0	8.9	9.1	8.9
Norway	18.4	17.8	16.1	16.2	18.3	15.3	16.2	11.7	11.1	10.6
Poland							17.5	14.0	13.8	14.1
Portugal[2]	41.5	33.8	27.0	27.2	28.7	23.4	17.0	14.3	14.2	
Slovak Republic[2]								13.4	10.1	10.8
Spain	18.4	15.5	8.7	10.5	13.0	10.5	10.3	10.2	9.8	9.7
Sweden	19.2	16.3	10.7	9.2	11.6	9.2	7.9	6.7	7.0	7.3
Switzerland	19.0	17.1	10.6	9.8	9.5	8.2	8.4	8.0	8.3	8.2
Turkey	53.4	48.8	40.9	25.2	12.4	7.3	6.0	16.4	15.6	19.1
United Kingdom	25.2	19.9	14.8	13.3	13.8	12.5	14.3	12.3	11.8	12.0
Unweighted average:										
OECD total	24.1	20.5	17.6	16.6	16.2	13.0	13.0	11.7	11.3	11.3
OECD America	16.0	12.5	11.8	18.6	23.3	17.1	17.7	16.1	15.6	15.0
OECD Pacific	22.1	19.5	23.8	21.8	20.5	14.6	13.2	12.3	12.8	12.2
OECD Europe	25.2	21.5	16.9	15.2	14.1	12.0	12.3	11.0	10.5	10.6
EU19	22.9	19.1	14.6	13.8	13.4	12.0	12.6	10.8	10.4	10.3
EU15	22.9	19.1	14.6	13.8	13.4	12.0	11.6	10.2	10.0	9.9

* These tables are taken from *Revenue Statistics* which are published annually by the OECD and are based on a nomenclature common to the OECD countries. Category 5110, which covers general taxes on goods and services, is used for Tables 3.1 and 3.2 and includes VAT/GST, sales taxes and other general taxes on goods and services. Category 5120, *Taxes on specific goods and services*, consists primarily of excise taxes, but also includes certain specific taxes such as customs duties and taxes on insurance and certain financial operations in particular. *Revenue Statistics 1965-2003* is for sale at the OECD's on-line bookshop: *www.oecd.org/bookshop.*

1. The tax revenues have been reduced by the amount of the capital transfer. The capital transfer has been allocated between tax headings in proportion to the reported tax revenues.
2. For the year 2002, provisional data published in the *Revenue Statistics* Edition 2003 are used.

Source: Revenue Statistics 1965-2003, 2004 Edition.

Table 3.5. **VAT/GST rates in OECD member countries**

	Standard rate					Reduced rate	Domestic zero rate[1]	Specific rate applied within specific region
	1994	1996	1998	2000	2003			
Australia	–	–	–	10.0	10.0	–	No	–
Austria	20.0	20.0	20.0	20.0	20.0	10.0 and 12.0	No	16[2]
Belgium	20.5	21.0	21.0	21.0	21.0	6 and 12.0	Yes	–
Canada	7.0	7.0	7.0	7.0	7.0	–	Yes	15[3]
Czech Republic[4]	n.a.	22.0	22.0	22.0	22.0	5	No	–
Denmark	25.0	25.0	25.0	25.0	25.0	–	Yes	–
Finland	22.0	22.0	22.0	22.0	22.0	8.0 and 17.0	Yes	–
France	18.6	20.6	20.6	20.6	19.6	2.0 and 5.5	No	0.9, 2.1, 8.0, 13.0, and 19.6[5] 1.05, 1.75, 2.1 and 8.5[6]
Germany	15.0	15.0	16.0	16.0	16.0	7	No	–
Greece	18.0	18.0	18.0	18.0	18.0	4.0 and 8.0	No	3.0, 6.0, 13.0[7]
Hungary[4]	n.a.	n.a.	25.0	25.0	25.0	12	Yes	–
Iceland	24.5	24.5	24.5	24.5	24.5	14	Yes	–
Ireland	21.0	21.0	21.0	21.0	21.0	4.3 and 13.5	Yes	–
Italy	19.0	19.0	20.0	20.0	20.0	4.0 and 10.0	Yes	–
Japan	3.0	3.0	5.0	5.0	5.0	–	No	–
Korea[4]	n.a.	n.a.	10.0	10.0	10.0	–	Yes	–
Luxembourg	15.0	15.0	15.0	15.0	15.0	3.0, 6.0 and 12.0	No	–
Mexico	10.0	15.0	15.0	15.0	15.0	–	Yes	10[8]
Netherlands	17.5	17.5	17.5	17.5	19.0	6	No	–
New Zealand	12.5	12.5	12.5	12.5	12.5	–	Yes	–
Norway	22.0	23.0	23.0	23.0	24.0	12	Yes	–
Poland[4]	n.a.	n.a.	22.0	22.0	22.0	7	Yes	–
Portugal	16.0	17.0	17.0	17.0	19.0	5.0 and 12.0	No	4.0, 8.0 and 13.0[9]
Slovak Republic[4]	n.a.	n.a.	23.0	23.0	20.0	14	No	–
Spain	16.0	16.0	16.0	16.0	16.0	4.0 and 7.0	No	2.0, 5.0, 9.0 and 13.0[10] 0.5 and 4.0[11]
Sweden	25.0	25.0	25.0	25.0	25.0	6.0 and 12.0	Yes	–
Switzerland	6.5	6.5	6.5	7.5	7.6	2.4 and 3.6	Yes	–
Turkey	15.0	15.0	15.0	17.0	18.0	1.0 and 8.0	No	–
United Kingdom	17.5	17.5	17.5	17.5	17.5	5	Yes	–
Unweighted average	17.1	17.2	17.7	17.7	17.8			

1. "Domestic zero rate" means tax is applied at a rate of zero to certain domestic sales. It does not include zero rated exports.
2. Applies in Jungholz and Mittelberg.
3. The provinces of Newfoundland and Labrador, New Brunswick, and Nova Scotia have harmonized their provincial sales taxes with the federal Goods and Services Tax and levy a rate of 15%. Other Canadian provinces, with the exception of Alberta, apply a provincial tax to certain goods and services. These provincial taxes apply in addition to GST.
4. The Czech Republic joined the OECD in 1995, Korea, Poland and Hungary joined in 1996 and Slovak Republic joined in 2000.
5. Applies in Corsica.
6. Applies to overseas departments (DOM) excluding French Guyana.
7. Applies in the regions Lesbos, Chios, Samos, Dodecanese, Cycladen, Thassos, Northern Sporades, Samothrace and Skiros.
8. Applies in the border regions.
9. Applies in Azores and Madeira.
10. Applies in the Canary Islands.
11. Applies in Ceuta and Melilla.

Table 3.6. **Annual turnover concessions for VAT/GST registration and collection**

	National currency	Registration thresholds in domestic currency[1]						Collection threshold (if different from registration threshold)[2]		Registration allowed prior to exceeding threshold[5]	Minimum registration period[6]
		General threshold		Reduced threshold for suppliers of services only		Special threshold for non-profit and charitable sector					
		Nat. curr.	USD	Nat. curr.	USD	Nat. curr.	USD	Nat. curr	USD		
Australia	AUD	50 000	28 075			100 000	56 150			Yes	1 year
Austria	EUR	22 000	23 102							Yes	5 years
Belgium	EUR	none						5 580[3]	5 860	Not applicable	None
Canada	CAD	30 000	19 082			50 000	31 803			Yes	1 year
Czech Republic	CZK	3 000 000	99 960							Yes	1 year
Denmark	DKK	50 000	7 071							Yes	None
Finland	EUR	8 500	8 926							Yes	None
France	EUR	76 300	80 123	27 000	28 353					Yes	None
Germany	EUR	16 620	17 453							Yes	5 years
Greece	EUR	9 000	9 451	4 000	4 200					Yes	5 years
Hungary	HUF	2 000 000	8 918							Yes	2 years
Iceland	ISK	220 000	2 724							Yes	2 years
Ireland	EUR	51 000	53 555	25 500	26 778					Yes	None
Italy	EUR	none								Not applicable	None
Japan	JPY	30 000 000	252 660							Yes	2 years
Korea	KRW	None								Not applicable	None
Luxembourg	EUR	10 000	10 501							Yes	5 years
Mexico	MXN	None								Not applicable	None
Netherlands	EUR	None						1 883[4]	1 977	Not applicable	None
New Zealand	NZD	40 000	20 963							Yes	None
Norway	NOK	30 000	4 332			140 000	20 217			No	2 years
Poland	EUR	10 000	2 605							Yes	Irrevocable
Portugal	EUR	none						9 975	10 475	Not applicable	5 years
Slovak Republic	SKK	3 000 000	75 990							Yes	1 year
Spain	EUR	None								Not applicable	None
Sweden	SEK	none								Not applicable	None
Switzerland	CHF	75 000	54 317			150 000	108 633			Yes	None
Turkey	TRL	None								Not applicable	None
United Kingdom	GBP	55 000	88 627							Yes	None
United States	USD	Not applicable		Not applicable		Not applicable				Not applicable	Not applicable

Table 3.6. **Annual turnover concessions for VAT/GST registration and collection** *(cont.)*

1. Registration thresholds identified in this chart are general concessions that relieve suppliers from the requirement to register for VAT/GST until such time as they exceed the threshold. Except where specifically identified, these thresholds also relieve suppliers from the requirement to charge and collect VAT/GST on supplies made within a particular jurisdiction. Relief from registration and collection may be available to specific industries or types of traders (for example non resident suppliers) under more detailed rules, or a specific industry or type of trader may be subject to more stringent registration and collection requirements.
2. A collection threshold may apply where a jurisdiction does not have a registration threshold. In these jurisdictions, all suppliers are required to register for VAT/GST, but will not be required to charge and collect VAT/GST until they exceed the collection threshold.
3. A supplier is allowed to voluntarily collect VAT/GST where their total annual turnover is less than the collection threshold.
4. This is a net threshold equal to VAT on total annual turnover minus input tax.
5. "Yes" means a supplier is allowed to voluntarily register and collect VAT/GST where their total annual turnover is less than the registration threshold.
6. Minimum registration periods apply to general concessions. Specific industries, types of traders, or vendors that voluntarily register may be subject to different requirements.

Source: OECD Tax Database.

Table 3.7. Departures from standard exemptions[1]

	Exemption other than "standard exemptions"	Taxation of "standard exemptions"
Australia	Specific basic food and beverages, child care, religious services, supplies of going concerns, water, sewerage and drainage, certain supplies of transport and related matters, precious metals, international mail, grants of freehold and similar interests by governments, cars for use by people with disabilities.	Domestic postal services, sporting services, cultural services excluding religious services, insurance and reinsurance excluding health insurance, gambling (including lottery tickets and betting), supplies of land (except certain supplies of farm land), commercial property and new residential property.
Austria	–	Letting (private housing).
Belgium	Legal services (including public notaries and bailiffs).	–
Canada	Child care, legal aid, ferry, road and bridge tolls, standard government services.	Lotteries and gambling, supply and leasing of commercial land and buildings, domestic postal services.
Czech Republic	Public television and radio, supplies of enterprises.	Cultural services.
Denmark	Passenger transport, burials, products of artistic work, travel agents.	Theatre and cinema.
Finland	Services of performers, copyright to literary and artistic works, certain transactions by blind people, public cemetery services, self-picked natural berries.	Postal services, cultural services, letting of commercial buildings in certain cases (optional).
France	Construction, improvement, repair and maintenance work on monuments, cemeteries and graves commemorating war victims undertaken for public authorities and non-profit bodies; new industrial waste and recyclable material; Commodity futures transactions carried out on a regulated market; Services rendered by resource consortia to their members composed of natural or legal persons that are VAT exempt or not subject to VAT.	Letting of immovable property, Full taxation for letting of developed immovable property and land for professional use; Option to tax for letting of undeveloped immovable property for professional use in certain circumstances and letting of land and buildings for agricultural use. Transport services for sick/injured persons in vehicles not specially equipped for this purpose and/or carried out by persons who do not have administrative certification.
Germany	–	–
Greece	Legal services, author rights, artists services, public radio and TV, supply of water by public bodies.	Cultural services (under conditions – admission to theatres, cinemas, concerts, etc.: lower rate).
Hungary	Public radio and TV broadcasting, mass sports events, services rendered by intermediaries (in case of exempt supply of goods and services), lending of buildings for education, sport and cultural purposes, transfer of creditors and ownership rights, compulsory social security insurance, public administration.	Safe transactions, dental care. Ttransport of sick or injured person when not part of the human medical care. The letting of immovable property which is not for housing purposes is taxed at 25%. Supply of buildings and land is taxed if it is not for housing purposes.
Iceland	Sports, passenger transport, authors, composers, burials, travel agents.	
Ireland	Passenger transport, broadcasting, supply of water by public authorities, admissions to sporting events, child care, funeral undertaking and travel agents/tour operators.	Long-term letting of commercial immovable property, supply of land and buildings.
Italy	Municipal passenger transport, burials.	Supply and letting of commercial land and buildings (standard rate). Residential housing taxed only when letby building enterprises (at lower rate of 10%).
Japan	Social welfare services, sale of certain kinds of equipment for the physically handicapped, public services, securities.	Hospital and medical care, education, insurance and reinsurance, financial services, supply of land.
Korea	Certain public transport, supply of water and coal, mineral oil used for certain purposes in agriculture and fishery, funeral undertaking. Certain personal services similar to labour.	Rental and supply of commercial buildings, commercial cultural services, gambling in licensed clubs.
Luxembourg	–	–
Mexico	The sale of magazines, gold and silver coins and shares; the exchange of foreign currency; retailing of gold bullion; authors' rights; public transport of passengers by land; agriculture, forestry and fishing activities.	Postal and insurance services except life and agricultural insurance. The letting of commercial buildings and financial services for consumer credits and personal credits. Only the letting of housing is exempt.
Netherlands	Burials, cremations, public broadcasting, sports clubs, the services of composers, writers and journalists.	Cultural services (mostly lower rate), letting of immovable property other than houses (only at combined request by letter and hirer), supply of immovable property (only at the combined request of supplier and purchaser), the use of sports accommodation.

Table 3.7. **Departures from standard exemptions**[1] *(cont.)*

	Exemption other than "standard exemptions"	Taxation of "standard exemptions"
New Zealand		Postal services; human blood, tissues and organs, hospital and medical care; transport of sick/injured persons, dental care; charitable work, certain fund raising events, education; non-commercial activities of non-profit making organisations (other than unconditional gifts); cultural services; sporting services, insurance and reinsurance (other than life insurance and reinsurance); letting of immovable property (other than residential accommodation); betting, lotteries and gambling; supply of land and buildings (other than land and buildings which have been used for the provision of residential accommodation for five years or more).
Norway	Passenger transport, burials, accommodation in hotels.	Postal services.
Poland	Agricultural services, taxi services, research and development services, funeral, cremation and cemetery services, public broadcasting, public television and radio, certain veterinary services.	Pawn activity except for service provided by banks, rental or tenancy of the dwelling immovable property used for commercial purposes.
Portugal	Agriculture.	
Slovak Republic	Public television and radio.	
Spain	Copyright to literature and works of art.	Some cultural services provided consumers pay for them.
Sweden	Public television and radio, authors' rights, public cemetery services, social services.	Postal services, most cultural services, letting of commercial buildings in certain cases (optional).
Switzerland	Taking care of children and young people under certain conditions, social services, social security services; provision of agency workers under certain conditions, certain second-hand goods.	Parking for cars unless additional to renting out of real estate, renting out of areas and individual rooms at fairs, certain bank services, provision of prosthesis and orthopaedic equipment.
Turkey	Deliveries and repairs of maritime, aircraft or railway transport vehicles used for business activities; social services; water used in agriculture.	Educational and cultural service, newspapers, books, magazines (lower rate), postal services, sale of commercial buildings, letting, radio and television broadcasting, hospitals, lotteries and gambling.
United Kingdom	Burials and cremations, sports competitions, certain luxury hospital care.	The freehold sales of new commercial buildings are standard rated for three years from completion date. Furthermore. there is an "option to tax" other supplies of commercial buildings which would ordinarily be exempt from VAT. Gaming machines and certain gambling in licensed clubs.

1. "Standard exemptions" are the following: postal services; transport of sick/injured persons; hospital and medical care; human blood, tissues and organs; dental care; charitable work; education; non-commercial activities of non-profit making organisations; sporting services; cultural services (except radio and television broadcasting); insurance and reinsurance; letting of immovable property; financial services; betting, lotteries and gambling; supply of land and buildings; certain fund-raising events.

Source: National Delegates; position as at January 2003.

Table 3.8. Coverage of different VAT rates[1]

	Zero rate	Lower rate
Australia	Specific basic food and beverages, health, child care, religious services, supplies of going concerns, water, sewerage and drainage, certain supplies of transport and related matters, precious metals, international mail, grants of freehold and similar interests by governments, farm land, cars for use by people with disabilities, exports and consumption outside Australia, supplies through inwards duty-free shops, education, non-commercial activities of charitable institutions and raffles and bingos conducted by charitable institutions.	–
Austria	–	Agriculture, books, food, forestry, hospitals, newspapers, art, culture, letting transport, supply of wine by farmers (12%).
Belgium	Cars for the handicapped, newspapers and certain weeklies.	Agriculture, food, water distribution, pharmaceuticals, books, works of art, collectors' items and antiques delivered by their authors/creators or their heirs, or imported, funeral services, devices for the handicapped, passenger transport, shows, hotels and camping sites, renovation of dwellings over 5 years old, private homes and establishments for the handicapped, subsidised institutional housing, coal and coke, some labour intensive services (small repair services.
Canada	Medicine, basic groceries, exports, certain financial services (usually to non-residents), certain agricultural and fishing products, medical devices, international travel and transport services, international organisations and officials, precious metals, (sales of 25 cents or less made through mechanical coin-operated devices).	–
Czech Republic[2]	–	Food, agricultural products, heating, personal transport, medicine, art, cultural service, laundry, books, newspapers, handicap equipment, most services.
Denmark	Newspapers.	
Finland	Subscribed newspapers and periodicals; printing services for certain membership publications; certain vessels.	Food, non-alcoholic drinks, animal feed, medicine, books, passenger transport, accommodation, TV licence, admission to cultural, entertainment and sporting events and cinema performances. Use of sports facilities. Works of art supplied by their creators or imported.
France	–	Medicine, handicap equipment, books, hotels, entertainment, Author's rights, museums, transport, accommodation, agriculture. Books, catering, newspapers, water, work on dwellings over 2 years old.
Germany	–	Food, books, newspapers, plants, flowers, devices for the handicapped, certain cultural events, museums, zoos, circuses. Charitable work if not exempt, author's rights, transport (only applies to passenger transport by ship and to local public passenger transport).
Greece	–	Electric energy, transport of passengers, food, water supply, medicine, handicap equipment, admission to shows, agricultural services, hotels, restaurants, sporting facilities, funeral services, authors and artists (if not exempt), books, press.
Hungary	Medicine for human consumption, books for public education, equipment for the blind and disabled (to be abolished on 1 January 2004).	Food, electric energy, books, equipment for the disabled, live animals, water, pharmaceutical products, mineral fuel for heating, newspapers, repairs of medical appliances, broadcasting, agricultural and fishery services, accommodation, transport, veterinary services, film services, art services, library services, bath services, funerals.
Iceland	International transport provisions, fuel and equipment delivered for use in ships and aircraft engaged in international traffic, ship-building.	Food, newspapers, books, hotels, warm water, electricity and fuel oil used for the heating of houses and swimming pools.

Table 3.8. **Coverage of different VAT rates**[1] *(cont.)*

	Zero rate	Lower rate
Ireland	Books, children's clothing and footwear, oral medicine, certain medical equipment, food products, seeds, fertiliser.	Newspapers and certain periodicals, fuel for certain purposes, electricity, works of art, veterinary services, agricultural services, car and boat hire, driving instruction, photographs, concrete, holiday accommodation, restaurant/hotel meals, building services, immovable goods, repair services, waste disposal, certain foods, tour guide services, admission to cinemas/certain musical performances and sporting facilities.
Italy	Scrap iron.	Food, medicine and health products/services for the handicapped, telecommunications, housing, books, newspapers, weekly publications, combustible gas for home heating, urban waste, purification stations, renewable-source energy, works of art, shows and transport. Accommodation let by building enterprises (10%).
Japan	–	–
Korea	Certain machinery and materials for agriculture, fishery, livestock and forestry, certain equipment for the handicapped.	–
Luxembourg	–	Accommodation, admission to cultural and sporting events, agriculture, author's rights, books, certain medical equipment, aids and other appliances normally intended to alleviate or treat disability, certain labour intensive services, children's clothing, construction of dwellings, electricity, foodstuffs for human and animal consumption, funeral services, gas, newspapers, passenger transport, periodicals, pharmaceutical products, renovation of dwellings over 20 years old, restaurant services, services supplied in connection with refuse collection and waste treatment, use of sporting facilities, water, works of art delivered by their authors/creators of their heirs, or imported.
Mexico	Sale of non-processed animals and vegetables (including wood in pieces) except rubber; patent medicines; milk, water, ice, food except processed food, smoked salmon and caviar; agricultural equipment, machinery and fishing boats; the wholesale of gold, gold bullion and jewellery; some agricultural and fishing services; the letting of some agricultural machinery and equipment; the export of goods and services; the sale of books and newspapers edited by the taxpayer himself; the provision of the water supply service for domestic purposes.	Sale of goods and services in the border regions.
Netherlands	–	Accommodation, agriculture, books, catering, food, goods and services for the handicapped, medicine, newspapers, magazines, passenger transport, water, entrance fees for sports events/amusement parks/museums/cinemas/zoos/circuses, restaurant/hotel meals, aids for the visually handicapped, use of sports accommodation, art and antiques, certain labour intensive services.
New Zealand	The supply of a taxable activity (business) as a going concern; the supply of fine metal (gold, silver or platinum) from a refiner in fine metal to a dealer in fine metal; the supply by a local authority of the local authorities petroleum tax (the distribution of the local authorities petroleum tax between local authorities.	For long-term stay in a commercial dwelling, certain services, if provided as part of the right to occupancy, are subject to tax at the standard rate on 60% of the value of the supply (an effective lower rate on such services of 7.5%).
Norway	Books; newspapers; certain aircraft and ships; transport services by ferrying vehicles; second-hand vehicles; electricity and district heating in the northern part of Norway, electric motor cars.	Food and public broadcasting (12%).
Poland	Basic agricultural means of production, books and specialised magazines, sea rescue services, goods and services supplied on ferries, goods designated for fire protection.	Goods for children, basic building material, some construction services, some goods connected with health protection, musical instruments, catering services, passenger transport, building of bridges, highways, certain hotel and restaurant services.

Table 3.8. **Coverage of different VAT rates**[1] *(cont.)*

	Zero rate	Lower rate
Portugal	–	5%: Essential foodstuff, water, medicine, devices for the handicapped, medical services (when not exempt), books, newspapers, electricity, passenger transport, admission to cultural and sporting events, natural gas, hotels and similar, social housing, some goods used in agriculture. 12%: Some other foodstuffs, restaurant services, diesel fuel for agriculture and heating oil, still wine, machinery mainly used in agricultural production, tools, machines and other equipment solely or mainly designed for collecting and using alternative energy sources.
Slovak Republic	–	Live animals; food; non-alcoholic drinks; water, coal, peat and coke; thermal energy; electric energy; gas; heating; wood for fuel; pharmaceutical products; exercise books; books; newspapers, magazines and periodicals; art; equipment for the handicapped; medicine; agricultur; hunting; forestry; fishery services; distribution of water, gas fuels and electricity; repair of shoes; hotel services; transport; services related to broadcasting and the transmission of TV and radio signals; research and development; legal services; architectural and engineering services; laundry services; public administration and defence; education; health and social welfare services; cleaning of waste water and solid waste disposal; recreation, cultural and sports activities; funeral services; some building services and building materials; transfer, transition and letting of immovable property.
Spain	–	Books, social accommodation, catering, certain cultural and entertainment services, food (for human and animal consumption) hotels, restaurants, supplies to the handicapped, medicines and other medical devices (*e.g.* lenses), transport, newspapers, public amenities, burial services, agriculture and forestry products used as food, goods used in agricultural and forestry undertakings, including flowers and plants, hairdressing and complementary services, minor work on private housing, cleaning, waste treatment, cleaning of public sewage, water, private and social housing, the supply of cleaning and maintenance services.
Sweden	Commercial aircraft and ships; aircraft fuel; prescribed medicine; printing of certain membership publications.	Accommodation, food, passenger transport, ski-lifts, newspapers, works of art owned by the originator, import of antiques, collector's items and works of art, culture (theatre, cinema, etc.), author's rights, books, newspapers, magazines, zoos, commercial sports events, commercial museums.
Switzerland	Certain supplies of goods and services to international airlines, supplies of some specific sorts of gold.	Water, food, medicine, books, newspapers, non-commercial television, accommodation, certain supplies in connection with agricultural production.
Turkey	–	Agricultural products, leasing, second-hand cars, newspapers, books, magazines, basic foodstuffs, natural gas, cinema, theatre, opera, ballet and education.
United Kingdom	Certain services and goods supplied to charities, children's clothing, food, passenger transport, books, newspapers, domestic sewage and water, prescribed drugs, medicine, certain aids and services for disabled people, new housing, residential and some charity buildings, alterations to listed buildings.	Fuel and power for domestic and charity use (5%). Certain energy saving materials supplied together with fitting services to recipient of "Passport Benefits".

1. Exports of goods, intangibles and services are generally zero rated in all OECD countries.
2. In Czech Republic a higher rate applies to cars, TV, washing machines, jewellery, road transport of goods, services of tourist agencies, accommodamtion, restaurant, repairs.

Source: National Delegates; position as at 1 January 2003.

Figure 3.1. **Standard rate of VAT at 1 January 2003**

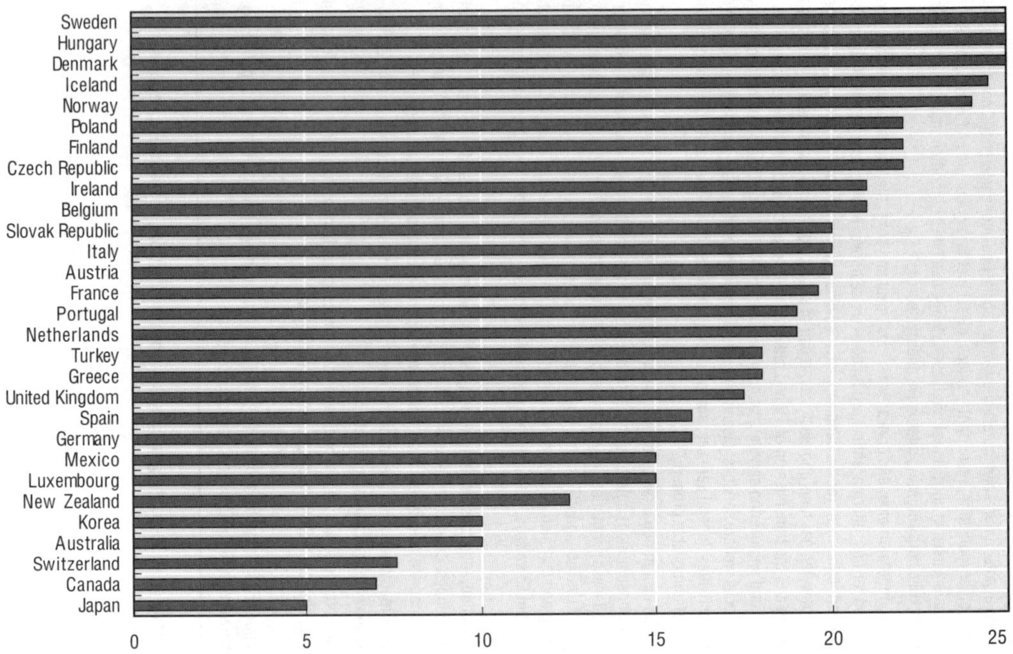

Source: National Delegates; position at 1 January, 2003.

vary appreciably and from this point of view the OECD member countries may be split into three broad groups:

- Ten member countries have a high threshold (more than USD 20 000): Australia, Austria, the Czech Republic, France, Ireland, Japan, New Zealand, the Slovak Republic, Switzerland and the United Kingdom.
- Ten member countries have an average or low threshold (between USD 2 000 and 19 999): Canada, Denmark, Finland, Germany, Greece, Hungary, Iceland, Luxembourg, Norway, Poland.
- Nine member countries have no general exemption threshold (even if some of them apply a threshold below which the duly registered taxpayer is exempt from applying the tax): Belgium, Italy, South Korea, Mexico, Netherlands, Portugal, Spain, Sweden and Turkey.

Table 3.9 shows the increasingly widespread use of reverse charging for cross-border supplies of digitised products between firms (25 member countries out of the 29 with VAT/GST). This method of taxation appears in both the OECD's 2001 Report on Taxation and Electronic Commerce (see Chapter I above) and the 6th VAT Directive of the European Union (19 members of which were in the OECD as at 1 May, 2004).

The same Table 3.9 also shows that more than two-thirds of member countries have systems of taxation on the margin between purchase and selling price. These systems apply mainly to travel agencies, second-hand goods (including antiques) andworks of art.

Table 3.9. **Special VAT taxation methods**

	Usage of reverse charge system	Usage of margin schemes
Australia	Imports of intangible supplies are reverse charged to the recipient (registered) business if they would not have been entitled to input tax credits for GST paid. Businesses can choose to reverse charge GST for supplies connected with Australia that are made by non-residents.	Optional GST on sales of new residential or commercial property based on the margin for the supply. Gambling: GST applies to the gambling margin calculated as total amount wagered less total monetary prizes awarded.
Austria[1]	Several services delivered internationally and intra-Community delivery of goods (EU Scheme); construction services: if the recipient of construction services is acting as general contractor or if he usually is rendering construction services the tax liability is shifted to him.	Travel agencies; second-hand goods, works of art, collector's items and antiques (EU Directive).
Belgium[1]	Several services delivered internationally and intra-Community delivery of goods (EU Scheme); some supplies of investment gold; work on immovable property (under several conditions) and for a number of transactions within the framework of a VAT warehouse; deferred payment scheme upon importation of goods into BE.	Travel agencies; second-hand goods, works of art, collector's items and antiques (EU Directive).
Canada	Resident business recipient of an imported taxable supply of intangible personal property or a service is required to self-assess tax in respect of the supply unless it is acquired for use, consumption or supply exclusively in the course of the commercial activities of the recipient.	No.
Czech Republic	EU Scheme applicable as at 1st May 2004.	Second- hand goods and travel agencies. EU Directive applicable as at 1st May 2004.
Denmark[1]	Several services delivered internationally and intra-Community delivery of goods (EU Scheme); goods imported B2B into Denmark from a country outside the EU; leasing of means of transport from outside the EU to a taxable person in Denmark.	No
Finland[1]	Several services delivered internationally and intra-Community delivery of goods (EU Scheme); If a foreign enterprise does not have a fixed establishment in Finland, the purchaser is usually liable for tax. Nevertheless, the seller is always liable to tax in the following cases: 1) the purchaser is a foreigner who does not have a fixed establishment in Finland and who has not been entered in the register of persons liable to value added tax; 2) the purchaser is a private individual; 3) in the case of distant sales of goods; 4) in the case of passenger transport, cultural, entertainment and educational services which are considered as sold in Finland.	Travel agencies; second-hand goods, works of art, collector's items and antiques (EU Directive).
France[1]	Several services delivered internationally and intra-Community delivery of goods (EU Scheme).	Travel agencies; second-hand goods, works of art, collector's items and antiques (EU Directive); Real estate agents.
Germany[1]	Several services delivered internationally and intra-Community delivery of goods (EU Scheme); if customer is an entrepreneur or a legal person governed by public law: – supplies of work and other services provided by an entrepreneur resident abroad (with the exception of certain services involving passenger transport); – supplies of pledged assets by the guarantor to the recipient of the security outside the framework of judicial liquidation; – (until 31.3.2004) supplies of real estate as part of execution proceedings.	Travel agencies; second-hand goods, works of art, collector's items and antiques (EU Directive).
Greece[1]	Several services delivered internationally and intra-Community delivery of goods (EU Scheme).	Travel agencies; second-hand goods, works of art, collector's items and antiques (EU Directive).

Table 3.9. **Special VAT taxation methods** *(cont.)*

	Usage of reverse charge system	Usage of margin schemes
Hungary	Financial, telecommunication sector, letting of properties (except immovable property), transfer of ownership rights in connection with copyright, patent, invention, trademark, etc., advertisement, legal, tax, accounting, computer, data processing etc. services, letting of manpower and personnel and the intermediate services of the above mentioned services. EU Scheme applicable as at 1st May 2004.	Yes, the resale of works of art, antiques, collectors' items, second hand goods, the marketing of waste materials, activities relating to tourism. EU Directive applicable as at 1st May 2004.
Iceland	No.	No.
Ireland[1]	Several services delivered internationally and intra-Community delivery of goods (EU Scheme).	Optional margin scheme for antiques, works of art and second hand goods. There is an obligatory margin scheme for auctioneers.
Italy[1]	Several services delivered internationally and intra-Community delivery of goods (EU Scheme); Investment gold: supply of semi-finished products, gold purity > 0.325, so-called industrial gold.	Travel agencies; second-hand goods, works of art, collector's items and antiques (EU Directive).
Japan	No.	No margin scheme (but a simplified tax system allowing particular S&M enterprises to calculate creditable CT figure by using deemed input/output ratio – 50-90% according to the type of business of the enterprises – notwithstanding that they get no input invoice.
Korea	Services which are provided by foreigners or foreign corporations that are not located in Korea, except in cases where the services received are used in taxable operations.	No.
Luxembourg[1]	Several services delivered internationally and intra-Community delivery of goods (EU Scheme).	Travel agencies; second-hand goods, works of art, collector's items and antiques (EU Directive).
Mexico	No.	No.
Netherlands[1]	Several services delivered internationally and intra-Community delivery of goods (EU Scheme).	Travel agencies; second-hand goods, works of art, collector's items and antiques (EU Directive).
New Zealand	No. Legislation was enacted in November 2003 implementing a reverse charge on business-to-business transactions. The new legislation has not yet taken effect.	No.
Norway	Taxable persons and public institutions that receive services capable of delivery from a remote location abroad are obliged to account for VAT under a self-assessment arrangement.	Voluntary margin scheme for second hand goods, works of art, collectors items and antiques.
Poland	Reverse charge system is applied to import of services (services rendered by foreign traders not established in Poland). EU Scheme as at 1st May 2004.	
Portugal[1]	Several services delivered internationally and intra-Community delivery of goods (EU Scheme).	Travel agencies; second-hand goods, works of art, collector's items and antiques (EU Directive).
Slovak Republic	No. EU Scheme as at 1st May 2004.	Special VAT scheme for travel agencies. EU Directive applicable as at 1st May 2004.
Spain[1]	Several services delivered internationally and intra-Community delivery of goods (EU Scheme).	Travel agencies; second-hand goods, works of art, collector's items and antiques (EU Directive).
Sweden[1]	Several services delivered internationally and intra-Community delivery of goods (EU Scheme).	Travel agencies; second-hand goods, works of art, collector's items and antiques (EU Directive).
Switzerland	The reverse charge system is applicable for the receipt of services taxable in Switzerland from enterprises with their place of business outside of Swiss territory.	Optional margin taxation scheme for used, individualised, movable goods for the purpose of resale, if a deduction of input tax on the purchase price was not possible or was not claimed. As such, goods are also deemed works of art, collectors' items and antiques (except precious metals and precious stones).
Turkey	No.	No.
United Kingdom[1]	Several services delivered internationally and intra-Community delivery of goods (EU Scheme).	Travel agencies; second-hand goods, works of art, collector's items and antiques (EU Directive).

1. "EU Scheme": within the European Union the person liable to pay the tax is in principle the taxable person carrying out the supply of goods or services. Nevertheless, several operations give rise to payment of VAT by the person to whom the goods or services are supplied (6th VAT Directive 77/388/EC). This is mainly the case for the intra-Community delivery of goods between taxpayers (art. 28c); several services listed in art. 9,2,e (advertising, transfers of copyrights, etc., consultants, engineers, accountants, banking, financial and insurance, supply of staff, services of agents, hiring out of movable tangible property, telecommunications, radio and TV broadcasting, electronically supplied services) and services included in article 28b of 6th Directive (intra-community transport of goods, services by intermediaries, valuations or work on movable tangible property).

Table 3.10. Import/export of goods by individuals

	Thresholds for tax-free import of goods by individual travellers			Refund for individuals upon export		
	Scheme	Max. threshold		Scheme	Min. value	
		Nat. curr.	USD		Nat. curr.	USD
Australia	AUD 400 worth of goods (or AUD 200 for people under the age of 18), 1.125 litres of alcohol and 250 cigarettes or 250 g of cigars or other tobacco products may be imported without individuals needing to be assessed for GST and customs duty. If the individuals have in excess of this amount, they need to declare goods and be assessed. However, if the total duty and tax payable is less than AUD 50, collection is waived.	AUD 400	225	Tourist Refund Scheme (TRS): individuals may claim a refund of GST on purchases made over AUD300 from a single business within 28 days of departure. GST refunds are available when goods are shown with the necessary documentation, on departure from Australia. The TRS applies to both residents and non-residents.	AUD 300	168
Austria	EU Scheme.[1]	EUR 175	184	Refund to individuals exporting goods in their personal luggage to a destination outside the EU minimum invoice amount EUR 75.	EUR 75	79
Belgium	EU Scheme.[1]	EUR 175	184	Refund to individuals exporting goods in their personal luggage to a destination outside the EU minimum invoice EUR 125.	EUR 125	131
Canada	I. Goods acquired abroad and for personal or household use imported by Canadian residents, temporary residents or former residents returning to live in Canada: – returning after an absence of not less than 24 hours, goods (except alcoholic beverages and tobacco products) valued at not more than CAD 50 and included in the baggage accompanying the person; – returning after an absence of not less than 48 hours, goods (including either wine not exceeding 1.5 litres or any alcoholic beverages not exceeding 1.14 litres and tobacco not exceeding fifty cigars, two hundred cigarettes, two hundred tobacco sticks and two hundred grams of manufactured tobacco) valued at not more than CAD 200 and included in the baggage accompanying the resident; – returning after an absence of not less than seven days, goods (including either wine not exceeding 1.5 litres or any alcoholic beverages not exceeding 1.14 litres and tobacco not exceeding fifty cigars, two hundred cigarettes, two hundred tobacco sticks and two hundred grams of manufactured tobacco)valued at not more than CAD 750 whether or not (except for alcoholic beverages and tobacco products) included in the baggage accompanying the person. II. Goods that are zero-rated when supplied domestically (for example, basic groceries). III. Conveyances and baggage temporarily imported by non-residents for use in Canada. IV. Casual donations valued at CAD 60 or under sent by persons abroad to friends in Canada or imported personally by non-residents as gifts to friends in Canada (except advertising matter, tobacco or alcoholic beverages).	CAD 750	477	Rebate is available to non-resident individuals who purchase eligible goods or eligible short-term accommodation while visiting Canada. Generally, eligible goods are those that are acquired by the individual primarily for use outside Canada, exported within 60 days of delivery to the individual and for which there is appropriate proof of export. Eligible goods exclude excisable goods and gasoline, deisel fuel and other motor fuels. Eligible accommodation is accommodation in a unit provided for less than one month of continuous occupancy. The total purchase amount for eligible goods and short-term accommodation (before taxes) must be at least CAD 200 and for eligible goods, each receipt must show a minimum purchase amount (before taxes) of CAD 50.	CAD 200	127

Table 3.10. **Import/export of goods by individuals** *(cont.)*

	Thresholds for tax-free import of goods by individual travellers			Refund for individuals upon export		
	Scheme	Max. threshold		Scheme	Min. value	
		Nat. curr.	USD		Nat. curr.	USD
Canada	V. Personal effects of seasonal residents VI. Personal effects of returning former residents (resident in another country for at least one year) or residents who have been abroad for at least one year (goods must have been actually owned, possessed and used abroad by the individual for at least six months prior to the individual's return to Canada and accompany the individual upon return to Canada). VII. Personal effects of settlers. VIII. Personal effects of settlers acquired with blocked currencies. IX. Foreign conveyances temporarily imported by a Canadian resident to be used in the international non-commercial transportation of the individual and accompanying the individual using the conveyance. X. Medals, trophies and other prizes that are: – won outside Canada or donated by persons outside Canada for heroic deeds, valour or distinction; – to be presented by the importer at awards ceremonies, or – bestowed or awarded abroad as marks of honour or distinction, won abroad in competitions, or won abroad in competitions and donated by persons abroad for bestowal or award in Canada					
Czech Republic	EU Scheme[1] as at 1st May 2004.	CZK 6 000	200	Refund to individuals exporting goods in their personal luggage to a destination outside the country minimum invoice CZK 1 000 for one seller on one day.	CZK 1 000	33
Denmark	EU Scheme.[1]	DKK 360	51	Refund to individuals exporting goods in their personal luggage to a destination outside the EU. Travellers from Norway and the Aland Islands can only get refund if the value of the goods exceeds DKK 1 200.	DKK 1 200	170
Finland	EU Scheme.[1]	EUR 175	184	Refund to individuals exporting goods in their personal luggage to a destination outside the EU, minimum invoice EUR 40. Traveller from Norway and the Åland Islands can only get the refund if the value of the goods without VAT is at the minimum EUR 170.	EUR 40	42
France	EU Scheme.[1]	EUR 175	184	Refund to individuals exporting goods in their personal luggage to a destination outside the EU.		
Germany	EU Scheme.[1]	EUR 175	184	Refund to individuals exporting goods in their personal luggage to a destination outside the EU. The traveller's habitual residence must be outside the European Community. The goods have to be exported within three months following the month of purchase. The VAT exemption is only valid for non-commercial purposes (except for the equipment and supply of private means of transport *e.g.* car, motorboat, aeroplane, etc.). The goods must be exported in the traveller's personal luggage.		

Table 3.10. **Import/export of goods by individuals** *(cont.)*

	Thresholds for tax-free import of goods by individual travellers			Refund for individuals upon export		
	Scheme	Max. threshold		Scheme	Min. value	
		Nat. curr.	USD		Nat. curr.	USD
Greece	EU Scheme.[1]	EUR 175	184	Refund to individuals exporting goods in their personal luggage to a destination outside the EU minimum invoice EUR 120. Limitations : alimentary products, alcoholic beverages, tobaccos, goods for the supply and equipment of private motor vehicles, aircrafts or sea-going vessels, goods having commercial character.	EUR 120	126
Hungary	EU Scheme[1] as at 1st May, 2004.	HUF 1 000	5	Refund to individuals exporting goods in their personal luggage to a destination outside the country. Minimum invoice HUF 50 000. Limitation: certain works of art, antiques and tobacco products.	HUF 50 000	223
Iceland	ISK 46 000 for travellers.	ISK 46 000	569	Refund for individuals when leaving the country for goods worth more than ISK 4 000.	ISK 4 000	50
Ireland	EU Scheme.[1]	EUR 175	184	Refund to individuals exporting goods in their personal luggage to a destination outside the EU. There is no threshold as to the amount.	–	–
Italy	EU Scheme.[1]	EUR 175	184	Refund to individuals exporting goods in their personal luggage to a destination outside the EU minimum threshold is fixed at EUR 154.93.	EUR 155	163
Japan	JPY 10 000 for individuals and corporations. Securities, postage stamps, revenue stamps, certificate stamps, commodity stamps, certain kinds of equipment for the physically handicapped, certain kinds of textbooks.	JPY 10 000	84	No. [Foreign travellers are exempted from VAT (only for goods, not for services) when they buy goods in tax-free shops and export them.]	–	–
Korea	Importation of the following duty-exempt goods under the Customs Law is exempted from value-added tax. Books, newspapers, and magazines. Duty-exempt goods of a small amount (KRW 100 000) imported by a resident. Goods imported from moving, immigration, or inheritance. Personal effects of travellers, or goods arriving by separate post and mailed goods that are exempted from customs duties or chargeable by the simplified tariff rates.	KRW 100 000	84	Foreign tourist who buys goods at VAT-free shop for foreign tourist and takes those abroad can be refunded.	–	–
Luxembourg	EU Scheme.[1]	EUR 175	184	Refund to individuals exporting goods in their personal luggage to a destination outside the EU minimum invoice EUR 74	EUR 74	78
Mexico	1) Administrative Rule No. 2.7.2 includes a list of items that may be introduced to Mexico as part of the baggage of international passengers residing abroad or in Mexico. 2) When arriving to Mexico by ships or aircrafts it is possible to introduce tax free good which value does not exceed USD 300 or its equivalent in national or foreign currency. 3) When arriving to Mexico in terrestrial means of transportation such amount shall not exceed USD 50.	MXN 3 120	300	No.	–	–

Table 3.10. **Import/export of goods by individuals** *(cont.)*

	Thresholds for tax-free import of goods by individual travellers			Refund for individuals upon export		
	Scheme	Max. threshold		Scheme	Min. value	
		Nat. curr.	USD		Nat. curr.	USD
Netherlands	EU Scheme.	EUR 175	184	Refund to individuals exporting goods in their personal luggage to a destination outside the EU minimum invoice EUR 136.	EUR 136	143
New Zealand	No charge for GST or duties is made if the realisable revenue on any one importation is less than NZD 50. In practical terms, this means that goods which only attract GST can be imported up to a value of NZD 399 before the revenue collection threshold is crossed. This threshold does not apply to excisable products above the following quantities: Tobacco: 200 cigarettes, or 250 grams of tobacco, or 50 cigars, or a mixture of all three weighing not more than 250 g. Alcoholic Beverages: 4.5 litres of wine or 4.5 litres of beer – one bottle containing not more than 1 125ml of spirits, liqueur, or other spirituous beverages. Other concessions: Personal effects: wearing apparel, footwear purchased while outside New Zealand for the intended use or wear of the traveller. Goods need to accompany the traveller when arriving in New Zealand. Other accompanying goods: Each traveller may import other accompanied goods up to a total combined value of NZD 700, free of duty and GST. Gifts: if value is less than NZD 110 – free entry, if more than NZD 110 – GST and duty applies on the value in excess of NZD 110. Multiple gift allowances are permitted provide that the separate identity of each recipient can be established. Heirlooms: Items bequeathed to a person in New Zealand may be imported free of all Customs charges.	NZD 700	367	No.	–	–
Norway	The threshold is NOK 6 000 for travel abroad for more than 24 hours. For travel abroad of less than 24 hours, the threshold is NOK 3 000. For alcohol and tobacco, special quantitative limits apply.	NOK 6 000	866	VAT refunds are available for tourists. For Nordic countries a higher value applies.	NOK 250	36
Poland	EU Scheme[1] as at 1st May 2004.	PLN 705	184	VAT refunds are available for tourists. Refunds are allowed on all kinds of goods except fuels. Refunds are possible on invoices with a value of PLN 200 or more.	PLN 200	52
Portugal	EU Scheme.[1]	EUR 175	184	Refund to individuals exporting goods in their personal luggage to a destination outside the EU minimum invoice EUR 50 In all cases, except equipment, fuelling and provisioning of private means of transport.	EUR 50	53

Table 3.10. **Import/export of goods by individuals** *(cont.)*

	Thresholds for tax-free import of goods by individual travellers			Refund for individuals upon export		
	Scheme	Max. threshold		Scheme	Min. value	
		Nat. curr.	USD		Nat. curr.	USD
Slovak Republic	EU Scheme[1] as at 1st May 2004.	SKK 7 273	184	Individuals can not ask for VAT refund in case of fuels, alcoholic beverages, tobacco and tobacco products and food. Refund to individuals exporting goods in their personal luggage to a destination outside the EU minimum invoice SKK 5 000.	SKK 5 000	127
Spain	EU Scheme.[1]	EUR 157	184	Refund to individuals exporting goods in their personal luggage to a destination outside the EU minimum invoice EUR 90.	EUR 90	95
Sweden	EU Scheme.[1]	SEK 1 597	184	Refund to individuals exporting goods in their personal luggage to a destination outside the EU minimum invoice SEK 200. Higher value for Norway and the Åland island.	SEK 200	23
Switzerland	Personal belongings* like clothes, toiletries, sports equipment, film-, photo- and video-cameras, music instruments, etc.; food and non-alcoholic beverages for the day of travel; alcoholic beverages and tobacco: 200 cigarettes or 50 cigars or 250 grams of pipe-tobacco and 2 l up to 15 degrees plus 1 l. over 15.0 degrees alcohol; goods for gift purposes or for private use up to CHF 300 per person. *Personal belongings means what residents take with them when leaving the country and what non-residents will use during their stay and re-export when going home.	CHF 300	217	There is no refund of VAT to any individuals by the Administration levying VAT, but an exemption of supplies of goods the invoice of which is at least CHF 400 if they are exported by the non-resident purchaser within 30 days after delivery to the latter.	CHF 400	290
Turkey	–	–	–	VAT refund to passengers who do not reside in Turkey for the purchasing goods taken to abroad. Minimum invoice : TRL 100 million.	TRL 100 million	62
United Kingdom	EU Scheme.[1]	GBP145	234	Refund to individuals exporting goods in their personal luggage to a destination outside the EU minimum invoice EUR 136. Threshold on refunds set by retailer.	GBP 89	143
United States	The allowance is USD 800 per person for absences over 48 hours, every 30 days, including up to 1 litre of alcoholic beverages, 200 cigarettes and 100 cigars. The goods must be for personal or household use only, or *bona fide* gifts, and not for the account of any other person, nor may they be re-sold. The amount may be pooled with family members. A traveller who has already used the USD 800 monthly allowance still has available a USD 200 exemption per crossing. This amount may not be pooled with family members, and if the value of the goods exceeds USD 200 the exemption does not apply and duties are levied on the total value of the goods imported.	USD 800	800	–	–	–

Table 3.10. **Import/export of goods by individuals** *(cont.)*

	Thresholds for tax-free import of goods by individual travellers			Refund for individuals upon export		
	Scheme	Max. threshold		Scheme	Min. value	
		Nat. curr.	USD		Nat. curr.	USD
European Union	EU Regulations allow tax-free import of goods from outside the EU by individuals for non-commercial purposes in their personal luggage to the extent that the global value of the imported goods does not exceed EUR 175. Nevertheless, special quantitative limits by traveller apply for the following high-duty goods (Regulations 69/169 – VAT and Excise – and 918/83 – Duties) : *a)* Tobacco: 200 cigarettes, or 100 cigarillos (cigars of a maximum weight of three grams each), or 50 cigars, or 250 grams of smoking tobacco; *b)* Alcoholic beverages: – distilled beverages and spirits of an alcoholic strength exceeding 22% vol.: 1 litre, or – distilled beverages and spirits, and aperitifs with a wine or alcoholic base, of an alcoholic strength not exceeding 22% vol.; sparkling wines, liqueur wines and still wines: 2 litres; *c)* Perfumes : 50 grams and toilet waters: 0.25 litre. Several additional limitations may apply for travellers under 15 years of age, persons residing in the frontier zone or frontier workers. Several goods may be admitted free of import duties and VAT according to the non-tariff exemptions of Regulation 918/83 (duties) and 83/181 (VAT), for example, educational, scientific and cultural materials, scientific instruments and apparatus, therapeutic substances, goods for charitable or philanthropic organisations, articles intended for the blind and other handicapped persons	175	184			

1. Thresholds and limits for VAT-free import of goods by individual travellers within the EU from non-EU Countries are defined by Council Regulation 918/83 of 28 March 1983. This customs regulation is explained under "European Union" at the end of this table.

ISBN 92-64-00676-1
Consumption Tax Trends
VAT/GST and Excise Rates, Trends and Administration Issues

Chapter 4

Selected Excise Duties in OECD Member Countries

Introduction

Before the introduction of general consumption taxes excise and customs duties were the recognised mean of taxing consumption. Unlike customs duties however excise duties are normally levied on all consumption of certain goods whether domestically produced or imported. Excise duties share with the Value Added Tax (VAT) the principle of neutrality towards goods produced abroad.

Excise duty, unlike VAT and general consumption taxes, is levied only on specifically defined goods. The three principal product groups, which remain liable to excise duties in virtually all OECD countries, are alcoholic beverages, mineral oils and tobacco products.

Before looking at these three groups in terms of their characteristics and comparative treatment by different tax administrations, a number of general characteristics on excise taxes may be noted:

- Excise charges are generally calculated using specific rates of duty on volume and/or content, combined in several cases with taxes (see Table 4.5).
- Excise duty, unlike VAT, does not normally become payable until the goods are entered into free circulation. Transfers of ownership can take place while goods remain in a controlled warehousing environment or between registered operators without creating an excise (or VAT) charge.
- As opposed to VAT, the excise system is characterised by a small number of taxpayers in the three main sectors at the manufacturing or wholesale stage.

Excise duties are normally part of the VAT tax base, meaning that VAT is usually levied on the duty-paid value of the excise products.

The main purpose and the original reason for the introduction of excise duties were to raise revenue on goods that were, at the time, regarded as non-essential. The nature of some of the products commonly subject to excise is such that the taxes are sometimes referred to as "sin taxes". In recent times, an alternative philosophy has emerged, recognising the application of excise duties as a means of influencing consumer behaviour.

The case put forward in relation to alcoholic beverages and tobacco products is that drinking and smoking are health hazards and increased excise duties help to reduce consumption.

For mineral oils reasons for determining consumer behaviour reflect a mixture of energy conservation, transport and environmental issues. Over the last decade, environmental issues have played an increasing role in determining the nature and application of excise duties to, in particular, road fuel.

Taxes on the purchase or use of motor vehicles (see Chapter V) and fuels, including petrol and diesel, generate most of the revenues from environmentally related taxes.

While the main characteristics and objectives ascribed to excise duties are approximately the same across OECD countries, their implementation, especially in respect to tax rates, sometimes gives rise to significant differences between countries. For example, excise on wine (Table 4.2) may vary from zero (Austria, Czech Republic, Germany, Greece, Italy, Luxemburg, Portugal, Slovak Republic, Spain and Switzerland) to USD 6.37 (Iceland) a litre.

However, the development of integrated markets (*e.g.* the European Union) and elimination of border controls at frontiers, has shone a light on the disparate excise rates between neighbouring countries to the extent that market forces are affected. This is not only true at the international level but often exists within a federal structure such as the USA where different excise rates apply in neighbouring states. In such circumstances the effects of cross-border shopping can have a significant economic impact on business in border areas and put pressure on the relevant tax authorities to seek closer approximation of excise duty rates with their neighbours.

Alcoholic beverages

In general terms, beer, wine and spirits are considered separate products within the category of alcoholic beverages. There are inevitably sub-divisions within each of these broad categories but the use of the internationally accepted Customs combined nomenclature code provides for consistency and helps to avoid contradictory definitions in applying rates.

Excise duties are applied to alcoholic beverages in two main ways. The duty can be either specific in relation to the alcoholic content of the product or and calculated on the basis of the value of the product; the two methods are sometimes combined to include an element of specific duty and an element. The effect of a specific rate is to penalise cheap or raw products (which may be more harmful to health) and to benefit the more expensive and mature products. The reverse can be said of an system and this is often the reasoning behind using a combination of the two methods. One exception is Mexico where a rate of duty alone is applied to alcoholic beverages, with that for beer graduated based on the alcoholic content of the product.

As with all forms of taxation inconsistencies do exist in relation to excise duties on alcoholic beverages. And although, in theory, excise duties should be neutral, preferential treatment and the use of tax rebates for local products can lead to distortion of competition in this field.

Tables 4.1, 4.2 and 4.3 in respect of excise duties on beer, wine and spirits illustrate, respectively, the complicated computations for excise duties and show the current comparative rates for OECD countries. Due to fluctuations in the value base, coupled with a mixture of specific and rates, it is difficult to be precise about the price differentials from a consumer point of view. What is apparent however is the obvious tax competition mentioned earlier between certain neighbouring countries giving rise to cross border "bootlegging" activities (*e.g.* UK/France and Denmark/Germany). Although some would argue that market forces should give rise to moves towards approximation of rates, this is contradictory with other policy factors when issues such as health have been taken into account in setting the rates. Figure 4.1 illustrates the vast spread of excise duty rates for wine and highlights the differences between northern and southern European countries. Figure 4.2 is a further endorsement of this fact with regard to spirits.

Figure 4.1. **Excise duties per litre of alc./vol.**

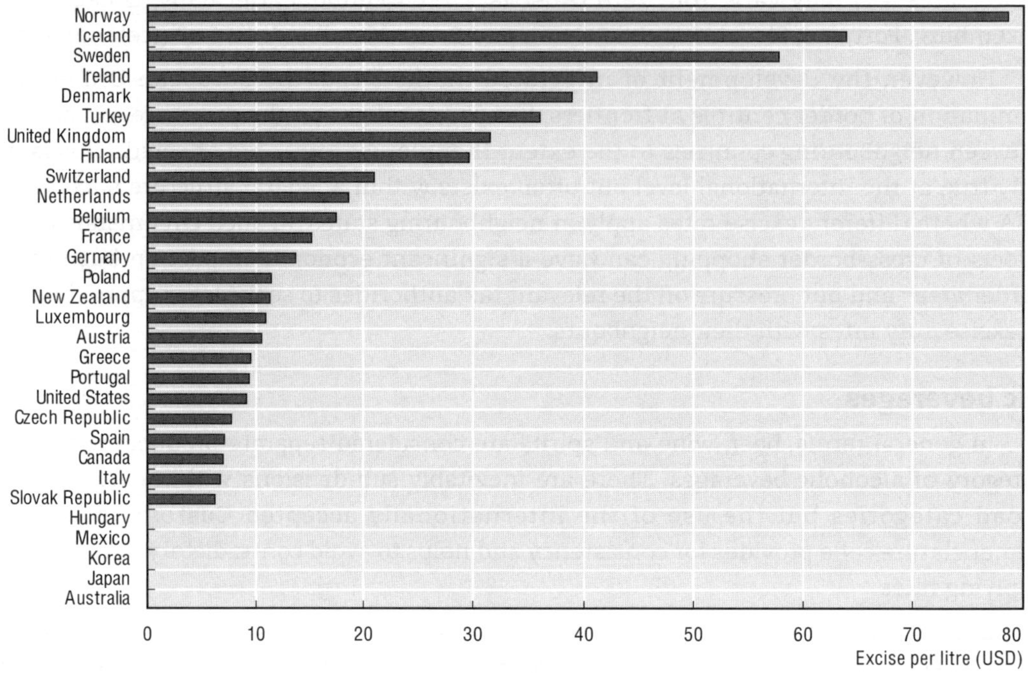

Source: National Delegates; position as at 1 January 2003.

Mineral oil products

Mineral oils are usually sub-divided into product categories in relation to technical specifications – leaded/unleaded petrol, diesel oil, heating oil and heavy fuel oil. Some OECD countries tax other energy products such as gas, electricity and coal but there is no common basis for taxing energy.

For social reasons nearly all OECD countries tax heating oil at a lower rate than diesel even though these two products are more or less identical. Only two OECD countries – Mexico and Turkey – have an tax on energy products. All other countries have a specific duty rate and no country has a combined system with a specific element and an element.

A much more significant feature of excise duties on mineral oils is the fact that duty rates have been used to affect consumer behaviour to a greater degree than in other areas. When the environmentally friendly unleaded petrol appeared on the market it was more expensive to produce and as a consequence not commercially competitive with leaded petrol as a retail product. This handicap was soon overcome through the use of tax differentials making unleaded petrol cheaper at the pump (see Chapter V). Nearly all OECD countries have adopted this approach, in combination with other non-fiscal measures such as making catalytic converters obligatory on new cars.

Table 4.4 gives the current rates for mineral oil products in OECD countries and again illustrates the wide disparity that exists in this area. The resultant price differentials are scrutinised more closely Chapter V.

Tobacco products

As with alcohol and mineral oils, there is a sub-division of tobacco products into a number of categories – cigarettes, cigars, cigarette rolling tobacco and pipe tobacco. For alcoholic beverages the objective criterion for excise duty is the alcoholic content; for mineral products it is the energy content. But what about tobacco – is there a smoking value difference between a cigar and a cigarette? Or should the nicotine/tar content be measured as part of the health issue?

Ostensibly for health reasons, most countries have tax differentials between cigarettes and other tobacco products making cigarettes relatively more expensive. However, unlike the success achieved with leaded and unleaded petrol, smokers do not see cigars and other tobacco products as substitutes for cigarettes, with the result that price elasticity in this field is much lower (near zero).

Although very few countries levy excise duties on alcoholic beverages and mineral oils on an basis alone, this method remains popular for tobacco products, particularly amongst members of the European Union. The majority of countries use a combination of specific and elements to calculate the excise liability on tobacco products. This not only helps to provide compensation in respect of cheap and expensive products (in much the same way as alcoholic beverages) but also acts as a means of achieving neutrality between countries with low production costs and those with high production costs. Those countries with low production costs might tend to choose a low specific element combined with a high element whereas high production costs can compensate by choosing a high specific element and a low element.

Table 4.5 shows the current excise rates for tobacco products in OECD countries. As with alcoholic beverages, the obvious price differentials contribute to cross border "bootlegging" activities.

Table 4.1. **Taxation of beer**

	Specific excise per hectolitre per degree Plato		Specific excise per hectolitre per degree alc.		VAT rate	Excise duty on low alcohol (under 2.8% alcohol by volume) beer Excise per hectolitre of product		Other features of the excise taxation system on beer	
	National currency	USD	National currency	USD	Per cent	National currency	USD	Excise rates which are progressive by strength	Low rates for small producers
Australia*	See note		See note		10.00	0.00	0.00	Yes	Yes – see note
Austria*	2.08	2.18			20.00			No	Yes
Belgium*	1.71	1.80			21.00			No	Yes
Canada*			27.99	17.80	7 or 15	See note		Yes	No
Czech Republic	24.00	0.80			22.00			No	Yes
Denmark*	268.50	37.97			25.00	0.00	0.00	Yes	Yes
Finland*			19.45	20.42	22.00	16.80	17.64	No	Yes
France			2.60	2.73	19.60	1.30	1.37	No	No
Germany*	0.79	0.83			16.00			No	Yes
Greece	1.13	1.19			18.00			No	No
Hungary	365.00	1.63			25.00			No	No
Iceland*			5870.00	72.67	24.50	0.00	0.00	No	No
Ireland*	–		19.87	20.87	21.00	See note		No	No
Italy	1.40	1.47			20.00			No	No
Japan*			See note		5.00			No	No
Korea*	See note		See note		10.00	See note		No	No
Luxembourg*	0.79	0.83	0.00	0.00	15.00	0.79	0.83	No	Yes
Mexico*			25%		15.00			Yes	No
Netherlands*	2.10	2.21			19.00			Yes	Yes
New Zealand*			See note		12.50	See note		No	No
Norway*			See note		24.00	See note		No	No
Poland*	6.86	1.79			22.00			No	Yes
Portugal*					19.00	6.19	6.50	Yes	Yes
Slovak Republic*	30.00	0.76			20.00			No	Yes
Spain*	See note				16.00	0.00		No	No
Sweden*			147.00	16.94	25/12	0.00	0.00	No	No
Switzerland	24.75	17.92	See note		7.60	See note		No	No
Turkey*			15.900.000*	9.86	18.00			No	No
United Kingdom*			11.89	19.16	17.50	0.00	0.00	No	Yes
United States*			21.00	21.00	–			No	Yes

Notes:

Australia. As at 1 January 2003, the excise rates for beer in individual containers not exceeding 48 litres are: AUD 29.36 per litre of alcohol where volume of alcohol does not exceed 3 per cent, AUD 34.22 where volume of alcohol exceeds 3 per cent but does not exceed 3.5 per cent or exceeds 3.5 per cent. The rates for beer in individual containers exceeding 48 litres are: AUD 5.86 per litre of alcohol where volume of alcohol does not exceed 3 per cent, AUD 18.41 where volume of alcohol exceeds 3 per cent but not 3.5 per cent, and AUD 24.09 where volume of alcohol exceeds 3.5 per cent. Each rate is calculated on the amount by which the alcohol content (by volume) exceeds 1.15%. Beer that does not contain more than 1.15% by volume of alcohol is free of excise. The wholesale sales tax of 37% was abolished from 1 July 2000. Though a microbrewery pays excise duty at the required rates, refunds are available to microbreweries meeting certain requirements.

Austria. Rates for small breweries (annual production up to 50 000 hl) range from EUR 1.24 to EUR 1.87 according to size of production.

Belgium. Rates for small breweries (annual production up to 200 000 litres of beer) range from EUR 1.4873 to EUR 1.6857 per hl per degree Plato, according to the size of production.

Canada. Excise rates are as follows per hectolitre of product: *a)* over 2.5% vol. CAD 27.985; *b)* over 1.2% vol. but not more than 2.5% vol. CAD 13.99; *c)* 1.2% vol. or less CAD 2.591.

Denmark. Excise rates are as follows per hectolitre of product: *a)* up to 11 degree Plato DKK 268.50; *b)* 11-14 degree Plato DKK 345.75; *c)* 14-18 degree Plato DKK 460.75; *d)* 18-22 degree Plato DKK 510.25; *e)* over 22 degree Plato DKK 27.00 per degree. Denmark has tax reductions for small breweries. The following rate applies on 1 October, 2004: DKK 58.40 per litre of pure alcohol. No duty on beer under 2.8% vol.

 CONSUMPTION TAX TRENDS – ISBN 92-64-00676-1 – © OECD 2005

Table 4.1. **Taxation of beer** *(cont.)*

Notes:

Finland. Four reduced rates for small independent breweries: *a)* EUR 9.73 (annual production up to 2 000 hl); *b)* EUR 13.62 (annual production over 2 000 hl and up to 30 000 hl); *c)* EUR 15.56 (annual production over 30 000 hl. and up to 55 000 hl); *d)* 17.51 (annual production over 5 500 hl and up to 100 000 hl.

Germany. Rates for small breweries (annual production up to 200 000 hl) range from EUR 0.3935 to EUR 0.5902 per hl per degree Plato.

Iceland. Excise rate in ISK 5 870 per % alcohol by volume exceeding 2.25%.

Ireland. Excise rate Nil below 1.5% ABV.

Japan. Excise rates are JPY 22 200 per hectolitre of product.

Korea. The current rate of Liquor Tax on beer is 100% of the manufacturer's price, and will be gradually lowered to 90% in 2005, to 80% in 2006 and to 72% in 2007. In addition to Liquor Tax, Education Tax is levied at varying rates on the amount of Liquor Tax. The rate of Education Tax on beer is 30% on the amount of Liquor Tax.

Luxembourg. Rates for small breweries (annual production up to 200 000 hl) range from LUF 16 to LUF 18.

Mexico. All rates are *ad valorem*. The rates for beer apply as follows: 25% up to 13.5° G.L.; 30% above 13.5° G.L. and up to 20° G.L.; 50% above 20° G.L.

Netherlands. For beer that is sold usually, that is, beer of 12 degree Plato in the range 11-15 degree Plato (EUR 25.11: 12 = EUR 2.10 per degree Plato). Excise rates are as follows per hectolitre of product: *a)* up to 7 degree Plato EUR 5.50; *b)* 7-11 degree Plato EUR 18.84; *c)* 11-15 degree Plato EUR 25.11; *d)* over 15 degree Plato EUR 31.40. Rates for small breweries (annual production up to 200 000 hl) are as follows: *a)* up to 7 degree Plato the above mentioned rate; *b)* 7-11 degree Plato EUR 17.43; *c)* 11-15 degree Plato EUR 23.23; *d)* over 15 degree Plato EUR 29.05. For beer with an alcohol content of. 0.5% the VAT rate is 6%.

New Zealand. The excise rate for beer containing more than 2.5% vol. is NZD 21.647 per litre of alcohol in finished product. The rate for beer containing more than 1.15% vol. but not more than 2.5% vol. is NZD 32.465 per hectoliter product. There is no excise duty on beer containing less than 1.15% vol.

Norway. Excise rates are as follows per hectoliter of product: *a)* 0.00-0.70% vol. NOK 155; *b)* 0.70-2.75% vol. NOK 243; *c)* 2.75-3.75% vol. NOK 918; *d)* 3.75-4.75% vol. NOK 1 589. The excise rate for beer with an alcoholic content of more than 7% vol is NOK 355 per degree of alcohol and hectoliter.

Poland. Allowances for small breweries: 20 PLN/hl if the producer sells no more than 20 000 hl a year. 10 PLN/hl if the producer sells no more than 70 000 hl a year. 8 PLN/hl if the producer sells no more than 150 000 hl a year. 6 PLN/hl if the producer sells no more than 200 000 hl a year.

Portugal. From 1 January, 2004, excise rates for beer are as follows per hectolitre of product: *a)* more than 0.5% vol. and up to 1.2% – EUR 6.19 ; *b)* more than 1.2% vol. and a degree Plato up to 8 – EUR 7.76; *c)* more than 1.2% vol. and a degree Plato in excess of 8 but up to 11 – EUR 12.39; *d)* more than 1.2% vol. and a degree of Plato in excess of 11 but up to 13 – EUR 15.52; *e)* more than 1.2% vol. and a degree of Plato in excess of 13 but up to 15 – EUR 18.59; *f)* more than 1.2% vol. and a degree of Plato in excess of 15 – EUR 21.75. Rates for small breweries (annual production up to 200 000 hl) are 50% of the normal rates.

Slovak Republic. Excise rate for small breweries (annual production up to 200 000 hl of beer) is SKK 23 per hectoliter per degree Plato.

Spain. Beer with an alcoholic content not exceeding 1.2% vol. is free of excise. The rate for beer between 1.2% and 2.8% is EUR 2.32 per hl; beer with an alcoholic degree > 2.8% and a degree Plato < 11 = EUR 5.34/hl; beer with a degree Plato > 11 and not > 15 = EUR 8.38/hl; beer with a degree Plato > 15 and not > 19 = EUR 11.43/hl; beer with a degree Plato > 19 = EUR 0.77 per hl. and per degree Plato. There is no tax on beer in Ceuta and Melilla – Spanish cities situated in the North of Africa.

Sweden. The rate shown is for beer stronger than 2.8% vol. The VAT rate for beer with an alcoholic strength lower than 3.5% vol. is 12%.

Switzerland. Uniform rate for all beers from 0.5 to 15.0 degrees alcohol.

Turkey. No specific tax element. The *ad valorem* elements are the Excise Duty at a rate of 63.3% No taxation according to the alcohol content. (*) If the amount of percentage tax is lower than the minimum amount of lump-sum tax computed according to the rate in the table for every alcohol degree, the minimum lump-sum tax is paid instead of percentage tax.

United Kingdom. Beer with an alcoholic content not exceeding 1.2% vol. is free of excise. Reduced duty rates apply for independent breweries producing no more than 30 000 hectolitres. For breweries producing between 5 000-30 000 hectolitres an arithmetic formula is used to determine the rate

United States. The weighted average Federal and State excise tax rate is USD 21 per hectolitre of product. The Federal tax is USD 18.00 per barrel (31 gallons). 26.42 US gallons = 1 hectolitre. Small domestic brewers who produce less than 2 million barrels of beer per calendar year pay USD 7.00 per barrel on the first 60 000 barrels. There is no progressive rate structure based on alcohol content and no Federal VAT.

Source: National Delegates; position as at 1 January 2003.

Table 4.2. **Taxation of wine**

	Still wine			Sparkling wine			Low-alcohol (still) wine (< 8.5% alc.)		
	Excise per hectolitre of product		VAT (%)	Excise per hectolitre of product		VAT (%)	Excise per hectolitre of product		VAT (%)
	National currency	USD		National currency	USD		National currency	USD	
Australia*	See note		10.00	See note		10.00	See note		10.00
Austria	0.00	0.00	20.00	144.00	151.21	20.00	0.00	0.00	20.00
Belgium	47.10	49.46	21.00	161.13	169.20	21.00	14.87	15.62	21.00
Canada*	51.22	32.58	7 or 15	51.22	32.58	7 or 15	See note		7 or 15
Czech Republic	0.00	0.00	22.00	2 340.00	77.97	22.00			22.00
Denmark*	705.00	99.70	25.00	1 055.00	149.20	25.00	450.00	63.64	25.00
Finland*	212.00	222.62	22.00	212.00	222.62	22.00	See note		22.00
France	3.40	3.57	19.60	8.40	8.82	19.60			19.60
Germany	0.00	0.00	16.00	136.00	142.81	16.00	51.00	53.56	16.00
Greece	0.00	0.00	18.00	0.00	0.00	18.00			
Hungary	500.00	2.23	25.00	7 930.00	35.36	25.00			
Iceland*	51 480.00	637.32	24.50	51 480.00	637.32	24.50	See note		24.50
Ireland*	273.00	286.68	21.00	546.01	573.37	21.00	90.98	95.54	21.00
Italy	0.00	0.00	10.00	0.00	0.00	20.00			
Japan	5 650.00	47.58	5.00	5 650.00	47.58	5.00			
Korea*	0.30	0.00	10.00	0.30	0.00	10.00	0.30	0.00	10.00
Luxembourg	0.00	0.00	12/15	0.00	0.00	15.00	0.00	0.00	15.00
Mexico*	25%/30%		15.00	25%/30%		15.00	25%		15.00
Netherlands*	59.02	61.98	19.00	201.24	211.32	19.00	29.51	30.99	19.00
New Zealand*	See note		12.50	See note		12.50	See note		12.50
Norway*	4 260.00	615.19	24.00	4 260.00	615.19	24.00	See note		24.00
Poland	136.00	35.43	22.00	136.00	35.43	22.00			22.00
Portugal	0.00	0.00	12.00	0.00	0.00	19.00			19.00
Slovak Republic	0.00	0.00	20.00	2 400.00	60.79	20.00	1 700.00	43.06	20.00
Spain*	0.00	0.00	16.00	0.00	0.00	16.00			
Sweden*	2 208.00	254.45	25.00	2 208.00	254.45	25.00	See note		25.00
Switzerland	0.00	0.00	7.60	0.00	0.00	7.60	0.00	0.00	7.60
Turkey*	150 000 000*	93.00	18.00	600 000 000**	372.00	18.00	150 000 000	93.00	18.00
United Kingdom*	154.37	248.75	17.50	220.54	355.38	17.50			
United States*	45.00	45.00	0.00	113.00	113.00	0.00	See note		0.00

Notes:

Australia. No distinction is made between still, sparkling or low alcohol wine, all are taxed at 10% by the Goods and Services Tax (GST) and all are liable for the Wine Equalisation Tax (WET). The WET was introduced on 1 July, 2000 to replace the difference between the previous 41% wholesale sales tax and the GST of 10%. The WET is levied at 29% of the wholesale value. The WET applies to the following alcoholic products provided they contain more than 1.15% by volume of ethyl alcohol: grape wine; grape wine products such as marsala, vermouth, wine cocktails and creams; fruit wines or vegetable wines; and cider, perry, mead and sake. From 1 October, 2004, a general rebate of WET applies to the first AUD1 million of production for each producer. The State Governments will also operate separate rebate/subsidy schemes in limited circumstances for cellar door sales.

Canada. A rate of CAD 0.5122 per litre applies to wine with an alcohol volume of more than 7% absolute ethyl alcohol by volume. The rate is CAD 0.2459 per litre on wine of more than 1.2% absolute ethyl alcohol by volume, but not more than 7%; and for all wine with 1.2% vol. or less the rate is CAD 0.0205 per litre.

Denmark. The rate for wine with more than 15% – maximum 22% volume is DKK 1055. Low-alcohol wine is more than 1.2% – maximum 6% volume. Still and sparkling wine is more than 6% – maximum 15% volume.

Finland. Excise rates for low alcohol wine are as follows: *a)* 5.5-8.0% vol. EUR 152; *b)* 2.8-5.5% vol. EUR 103; *c)* 1.2-2.8% vol. EUR 4.54.

Iceland. Excise rate shown in the Table is the rate for wine with 12% vol. The rate is ISK 5 280 per % alcohol by volume exceeding 2.25%.

Ireland. The rate for low alcohol wine applies to wine with an alcoholic content of less than 5.5% vol.

Korea. The rate of liquor tax on wine is 30% on the manufacturer's price and the rate of Education Tax is 10% of the amount of liquor tax levied. These rates are applicable to both still and sparkling wine regardless of alcohol content.

Mexico. All rates are *ad valorem*.

Table 4.2. **Taxation of wine** *(cont.)*

Notes:

Netherlands. Excise rate for low alcohol sparkling wine is EUR 38.16. For low alcohol wine < 5% the VAT rate is 6%.

New Zealand. The excise rate for grape wine is NZD 216.47 per hectolitre of product.

Norway. The rate shown in the Table is the rate for wine with an alcoholic content of 12% vol. Excise rates for wine with an alcoholic content of 4.76%-22% vol. = NOK 355 per vol. pct. alcohol and per hectoliter.

Spain. Intermediate products – products to which distilled alcohol has been added – and with a volume of alcoholic degree between 1.2% vol. and less than 22% are taxed according to the following rates: Alcoholic degree > 1.2% and less than 15% = EUR 27.50 per hl. Others = EUR 45.83 per hl.

Sweden. Excise rates for low alcohol wine are as follows: *a)* 7%-8.5% vol. SEK 1 541; *b)* 4.5%-7% vol. SEK 1 120; *c)* 2.25%-4.5% vol. SEK 758. No special rates for sparkling wine.

Turkey. No specific tax element. The *ad valorem* elements are the Excise Duty at rate of 63.3% or 275.6%. (*) The tax rate is 63.3%. But if the computed tax amount according to this rate is lower than the minimum lump-sum tax amount stated in the table, the minimum lump-sum tax is paid instead of percentage tax. (**) The tax rate is 275.6%. But if the computed tax amount according to this rate is lower than the minimum lump-sum tax amount, the minimum lump-sum tax is paid instead of percentage tax.

United Kingdom. Reduced excise rates for lower strength drinks (wine categories) are as follows: *a)* exceeding 1.2% – not exceeding 4% alcohol by volume = GBP 47.58 per hl; *b)* exceeding 4% – not exceeding 5.5% alcohol by volume = GBP 65.42 per hl; and *c)* low strength sparkling wine exceeding 5.5% – less than 8.5% = GBP 166.70 per hl. There is also a rate of duty in the band exceeding 15% but not exceeding 22%: GBP 208.52 per hl (wine and made wine). The United Kingdom also charges excise duty on cider and perry products. The following rates per hl applied on 1 January 2003: exceeding 1.2% but not exceeding 7.5%: GBP 25.61; exceeding 7.5% but less than 8.5%: GBP 38.43. Sparkling wine and perry – Exceeding 5.5% but less than 8.5%: GBP 166.70. Any still cider product which has a strength of 8.5% and over is dutied as a made wine.

United States. The weighted average Federal and State excise tax rate is USD 45 per hectolitre of product for still wine up to 14% vol., and USD 113 for sparkling wine. The Federal excise rates are as follows: *a)* up to 14% vol. USD 1.07 per gallon; *b)* 14%-21% vol. USD 1.57 per gallon; *c)* 21%-24% vol. USD 3.15 per gallon; *d)* artificially carbonated wine USD 3.30 per gallon; and *e)* sparkling wine USD 3.40 per gallon. 26.42 US gallons = 1 hectolitre. There is no Federal VAT.

Source: National Delegates; position as at 1 January 2003.

Table 4.3. **Taxation of alcoholic beverages**

	Tax per hectolitre of absolute alcohol			
	Excise		VAT	Small distillery rate
	National currency	USD	Per cent	
Australia*	See note		10.00	No
Austria*	1 000.00	1 050.10	20.00	Yes
Belgium	1 660.89	1 744.10	21.00	No
Canada*	1 106.60	703.85	7 or 15	No
Czech Republic	23 400.00	779.69	22.00	No
Denmark*	27 500.00	3 889.05	25.00	No
Finland*	2 825.00	2 966.53	22.00	No
France	1 450.00	1 522.65	19.60	No
Germany*	1 303.00	1 368.28	16.00	Yes
Greece*	908.00	953.49	18.00	No
Hungary*	1 670.00	7.45	25.00	No
Iceland*	516 120.00	6 389.57	24.50	No
Ireland*	3 925.00	4 121.64	21.00	No
Italy	645.36	677.69	20.00	No
Japan*	See note		5.00	No
Korea*	See note		10.00	No
Luxembourg	1 041.14	1 093.30	15.00	No
Mexico*	60%		15.00	No
Netherlands*	1 775.00	1 863.93	19.00	No
New Zealand*	2 164.70	1 134.45	12.50	No
Norway	54 400.00	7 855.90	24.00	No
Poland	4 400.00	1 146.20	22.00	No
Portugal*	898.12	943.12	19.00	Yes
Slovak Republic	25 000.00	633.25	20.00	No
Spain*	685.15	719.48	16.00	Yes
Sweden	50 141.00	5 778.25	25.00	No
Switzerland*	2 900.00	2 100.24	7.60	No
Turkey*	5 813 000 000.00	3 604.06	18.00	No
United Kingdom*	1 956.00	3 151.90	17.50	No
United States*	920.00	920.00	–	No

Notes:

Australia. As at 1 January 2003, the excise duty rate of AUD 57.97 per litre of alcohol applied to fruit brandy, whisky, rum, liquers and other excisable beverages (but not beer) of alcoholic strength exceeding 10 per cent. Brandy attracted the rate of AUD 54.13 per litre of alcohol and a lower rate of AUD 34.22 per litre of alcohol applied to other excisable beverages (but not beer) of alcoholic strength not exceeding 10 per cent.

Austria. The rate for small distilleries is EUR 540.

Canada. Spirits are subject to excise duty at the rate of CAD 11.066 per litre of absolute ethyl alcohol by volume. Spirits containing not more than 7% absolute ethyl alcohol by volume are subject to excise duty at the rate of CAD 0.2459 per litre.

Denmark. Tax was reduced to DKK 15.000 per hectolitre of pure alcohol as of 1 October, 2003.

Finland. Excise rates are as follows: *a)* CN – code 2208. alcoholic content between 1.2% and 2.8% vol. EUR 168; *b)* Other products EUR 2 825.

Germany. The rates for small distilleries are EUR 730 or EUR 1 022.

Greece. The rate for ouzo and ethyl alcohol (derogation possible for several regions but only applied in the department of Dodecanese) is EUR 454.

Hungary. Reduced rate (HUF 770) applies to ethyl-alcohol produced by fruit growers' distilleries from fruit supplied to them by private fruit growers. The application of reduced rate is limited to 50 litres of pure alcohol for private consumption per fruit grower per year.

Iceland. Excise rate is ISK 5 280 per % alcohol by volume exceeding 2.25%.

Ireland. Reduced rate of excise duty on spirits with an alcoholic content under 5.5% abolished from 05.12.02.

Japan. Excise rates are as follows: *a)* Whisky and brandy (40% vol.) JPY 40 900; *b)* Spirits (37% vol.) JPY 36 718.8; *c)* Shochu Group A and B (25% vol.) JPY 24 810.

Korea. As Excise Tax for liquor is based on the *ad valorem* system, the rate does not vary with alcohol content. For whisky, brandy, general distilled spirits, liqueur, diluted soju and distilled soju, the Liquor tax is 72% and the Education tax is 30%.

Table 4.3. **Taxation of alcoholic beverages** *(cont.)*

Notes:

Mexico. The rate is *ad valorem*. There is a charge per litre of alcoholic beverages produced, bottled or imported, which is levied on the first sale. The excise amount varies according to the type of drink and it is adjusted every month according to the change in the National Alcoholic Beverages Price Index. This charge is final in all cases. The charges per litre for some specific liquors are: *a)* Cognac MXN 858.10; *b)* Whisky MXN 63.95; *c)* Tequila MXN 43.68; *d)* Brandy MXN 22.62; *e)* Ron MXN 18.81; Others (from MXN 881.25 to MXN 4.3).

Netherlands. For low alcohol spirits with an alcoholic content < 1.2% the VAT rate is 6%.

New Zealand. For alcholic beverages with 0-14% alcoholic content, the excise rate is NZD 2164.70 per hectolitre of absolute alcohol. For alcoholic beverages above 14% in alcoholic content, the excise rate is NZD 3942.60 per hectolitre of absolute alcohol (with the exception of wine and vermouth which has the rate of NZD 216.47 per hectolitre of product.

Portugal. A reduced rate for small distilleries has applied since 14 February 1995.

Spain. The excise rate in the Canary Islands is EUR 494.06 per Hl of pure alcohol. There is a special regime for small distilleries for which the rate is EUR 599.57 per Hl (or EUR 466.82 in the Canary Islands).

Switzerland. Weighted average rate.

Turkey. No specific tax element. The *ad valorem* element is the Excise Duty at a rate of 275.6%. If the tax computed according to the tax rate is lower than the minimum tax amount specified in the official table, the minimum tax amount is paid.

United Kingdom. All drinks over 22% are dutied as spirits.

United States. The weighted average Federal and State excise tax rate is USD 920 per hectolitre. The Federal excise rate is USD 13.50 per proof gallon in 2003. A proof gallon is a US gallon (3.785 litres) containing 50% alcohol. There is no Federal VAT.

Source: National Delegates; position as at 1 January 2003.

Table 4.4. Taxation of mineral oils (per 1 000 litres of product at 15 °C)

	Leaded petrol			Unleaded petrol			Diesel			Industrial use of diesel[1]			Heating gas oil		
	Excise		VAT	Excise		VAT	Excise		VAT	Excise		VAT	Excise		VAT
	National currency	USD	Per cent	National currency	USD	Per cent	National currency	USD	Per cent	National currency	USD	Per cent	National currency	USD	Per cent
Australia*	See note		10.00	381.43	214.17	10.00	381.43	214.17	10.00	See note		10.00	75.57	42.43	10.00
Austria	479.00	503.00	20.00	407.00	427.39	20.00	282.00	296.13	20.00	282.00	296.13	20.00	69.00	72.46	20.00
Belgium*	551.81	579.46	21.00	493.56	518.28	21.00	290.04	304.57	21.00	18.59	19.52	21.00	5.00	5.25	21.00
Canada	110.00	69.97	7 or 15	100.00	63.61	7 or 15	40.00	25.44	7 or 15	40.00	25.44	7 or 15	0.00	0.00	7 or 15
Czech Republic*	10 840.00	361.19	22.00	10 840.00	361.19	22.00	8 150.00	271.56	22.00	8 150.00	271.56	22/5	0.00	0.00	22.00
Denmark*	4 651.00	657.74	25.00	4 006.00	566.53	25.00	2 734.00	386.64	25.00	2 087.00	295.14	25.00	2 087.00	295.14	25.00
Finland*	669.40	702.94	22.00	619.70	650.75	22.00	342.40	359.55	22.00	67.10	70.46	22.00	67.10	70.46	22.00
France*	–		–	589.20	618.72	19.60	391.90	411.53	19.60	566.00	594.36	19.60	566.00	594.36	19.60
Germany*	721.00	757.12	16.00	654.50	687.29	16.00	470.40	493.97	16.00	470.40	493.97	16.00	61.35	64.42	16.00
Greece*	337.00	353.88	18.00	296.00	310.83	18.00	245.00	257.27	18.00	245.00	257.27	18.00	245.00	257.27	18.00
Hungary	111 800.00	498.52	25.00	103 500.00	461.51	25.00	85 000.00	379.02	25.00	85 000.0	379.02	25.00		379.02	25.00
Iceland*	40 930.00	506.71	24.50	39 100.00	484.06	24.50	0.00	0.00	24.50	0.00	0.00	24.50	0.00	0.00	14.00
Ireland*	511.72	537.36	21.00	401.36	421.47	21.00	326.73	343.10	21.00	47.36	49.73	21.00	47.36	49.73	12.50
Italy*	541.84	568.99	20.00	541.84	568.99	20.00	403.21	423.41	20.00	61.75	64.84	20.00	128.61	135.05	20.00
Japan	55 840.00	470.28	5.00	55 840.00	470.28	5.00	34 140.00	287.53	5.00	2 040.00	17.18	5.00	2 040.00	17.18	5.00
Korea*	743 930.00	627.65	10.00	743 930.00	627.65	10.00	391 760.00	330.53	10.00	391 760.00	330.53	10.00		149.42	10.00
Luxembourg	424.14	445.39	15.00	381.08	400.17	12.00	252.83	265.50	15.00	18.59	19.52	15.00	5.00	5.25	12.00
Mexico*	0.69	0.07	15.00	0.71	0.07	15.00	0.56	0.05	15.00	0.63	0.06	15.00			
Netherlands*	703.67	738.92	19.00	616.48	647.37	19.00	337.25	354.15	19.00	46.56	48.89	19.00	46.56	48.89	19.00
New Zealand*	See note			362.00	189.71	12.50	0.00	0.00	12.50	0.00	0.00	12.50	0.00	0.00	12.50
Norway*	5 470.00	789.92	24.00	4 640.00	670.06	24.00	3 330.00	480.89	24.00	500.00	72.21	24.00	898.00	129.68	24.00
Poland*	1 672.00	435.56	22.00	1 498.00	390.23	22.00	See note		22.00	See note		22.00	195.00	50.80	22.00
Portugal*	548.68	576.17	19.00	522.60	548.78	19.00	308.29	323.74	19.00	308.29	323.74	19.00	89.65	94.14	12.00
Slovak Republic*	14 500.00	367.29	20.00	12 400.00	314.09	20.00	11 800.00	298.89	20.00	–		–	–		–
Spain*	404.79	425.07	16.00	371.69	390.31	16.00	264.99	278.27	16.00	78.71	82.66	16.00	78.71	82.66	16.00
Sweden*	5 400.00	622.30	25.00	4 710.00	542.78	25.00	3 178.00	366.23	25.00	3 178.00	366.23	25.00	2 894.00	333.50	25.00
Switzerland*				731.20	529.55	7.60	758.70	549.47	7.60	172.80	125.15	7.60	3.00	2.17	7.60
Turkey	818 000 000.00	507.16	18.00	848 000 000.00	525.76	18.00		376.30	18.00	256 544 000.00	159.06	18.00		159.06	18.00
United Kingdom*	562.00	905.61	17.50	471.00	758.97	17.50	471.00	758.97	17.50	42.20	68.00	17.50	42.20	68.00	17.50
United States*	112.80	112.80	–	112.80	112.80	–	127.86	127.86	–	0.00	0.00	–	0.00	0.00	–

Table 4.4. **Taxation of mineral oils (per 1 000 litres of product at 15 °C)** *(cont.)*

1. **Industrial use of diesel.** Diesel used for stationary motors, plants and machinery in construction, civil engineering and public works, and for vehicles intended for use off the public highway.

Australia. Leaded petrol has been superseded by Lead Replacement Petrol that is classified, for the purposes of excise duty, as unleaded petrol. The Energy Grants (Credits) Scheme provides excise relief to businesses through payment of a grant for diesel fuel used in eligible off and on-road activities. The overall objective of the scheme is to remove the incidence of fuel taxation on business inputs to production. The scheme provides full excise relief for diesel fuel (and "like" fuels) used in a limited range of off-road activities (including primary production, mining operations, rail and marine transport, hospitals, nursing homes and electricity generation at hospitality/retail premises) and partial excise relief for diesel fuel used in on-road vehicles over 4.5 tonnes gross vehicle mass.

Belgium. The excise figure of EUR 5 for heating oil is in fact a fee. In addition, unleaded petrol is subject to an energy contribution of EUR 13.6341; heating oil is subject to an energy contribution of EUR 8.4284 per 1 000 litres.

Czech Republic. For Industrial use of diesel, there is a refund for agricultural purposes of 60%. For Industrial use of biodiesel, the VAT rate is 5%. Mixture of petrol and alcohol or 15% ethil-tercial-butyl-ether is submitted to the same taxation as petrol. Fuels and lubricants used for air transport are exempt from excise duty.

Denmark. The rates for petrol are from service stations where a specific system has been installed, by which the greater part of the petrol fumes is lead back to the service stations' tank and re-used. The rates are 3 ore/l extra if not using this system. The rates include a 26.8 ore/l CO_2 tax. There exist reduced rates for energy used in energy-intensive processes. The rate for diesel is for low sulphur (max 0.005%). Diesel light: DKK 2 913. Diesel normal: DKK 3 012.

Finland. For environmentally friendly products, the rates are as follows: leaded petrol EUR 660.5, unleaded petrol EUR 580.8 and diesel EUR 315.9. There is a strategic stockpile fee of EUR 6.80 for petrol and EUR 3.50 for diesel and heating oil.

France. As of 1 January 2000, leaded petrol is no longer sold. Petrol with specific additives USD 668.10 /1 000 L.

Germany. Diesel used for stationary motors: EUR 61.36/VAT 16%.

Greece. 1) Unleaded petrol: < = 96.5 oct. Excise: EUR 296/ > = 96.5 oct. Excise: EUR 316. 2) A winter period is defined in Greece, each year (~ 1 November to April the following year). The normal rate of duty for the Winter period is EUR 123. During the winter period from 14/10/2002 to 25/4/2003 a reduced rate of EUR 18 was applied.

Iceland. Excise Duty on petrol is ISK 40 930 (leaded petrol) ISK 39 100 (unleaded petrol) per 1 000 litres.

Ireland. A higher rate of duty of EUR 453.58 per 1 000 litres applies to super-unleaded petrol.

Italy. The excise figure shown for industrial use of diesel only concerns diesel used for stationary motors, civil engineering and public works: it is not intended for plants and machinery in construction and vehicles to be used off the public road. As regards heating oil, the excise figure shown above refers to the cited fuel with a sulphur content higher than 1%. The excise duty for diesel for heating is EUR 403.21/1 000 l. Excise duty on petrol was increased to EUR 558.64/1 000 l as of 29.12.2003.

Korea. The figures above include the Education Tax (15% of the amount of excise Tax).

Mexico. All rates are *ad valorem* and vary monthly according to international petrol prices.

Netherlands. A reduced VAT-rate of 6% is applied to the supply of gas and heating gas oil used for the growth of horticultural products. Apart from the excise duties on mineral oils and within the framework of the law on environmental taxes, the Netherlands has energy taxes based on a 50% energy content/50% CO_2 component. The fuel tax has existed in one form or another since 1988 and covers fossil fuels used in combustion, at a fairly low tariff. The regulatory energy tax was introduced in 1996 and covers non-transport energy consumption; the tax base is limited to 1 000 000 m^3 of natural gas and 10 000 000 kWh electricity per year. Furthermore, a strategic storage levy is charged on some mineral oil products. Its purpose is the financing of the strategic oil reserves.

New Zealand. Does not refine or import leaded petrol.

Norway. The petrol tax rate shown includes a CO_2 tax of NOK 750/1 000 litres. The diesel tax rate shown consists of a tax on mineral oil used as propellant [varies with sulphur content: 0.000-0.005 weight per cent NOK 2 830/1 000 litres; above 0.005 weight per cent NOK 3 170/1 000 litres (the former is used in the table)] and a CO_2 tax of NOK 500/1 000 litres. The diesel tax rate for industrial use shown consists of a CO_2 tax of NOK 500/1 000 litres. The heating gas oil tax rate includes a CO_2 tax of NOK 500/1 000 litres. In addition, there is a SO_2 tax of NOK 70/1 000 litres and per 0.25 weight per cent sulphur content on mineral oils with 0.05 weight per cent sulphur content and over.

Poland. Varies with sulphur content: PLN 1 129; from 0.005% to 0.035% (sulphur content) – PLN 1 051/1000 l; from 0.005% inclusive – PLN 1 003.

Portugal. Data on 4 April 2000. Heating oil has existed in Portugal since 1st January 2003. Rates vary throughout the year, depending on international crude oil prices, within a range stipulated by law. Portugal has diesel for agriculture: rate EUR 76.04 per 1 000 L and VAT 12%.

Slovak Republic. Lower rate on gas oil marked for fiscal purposes, used for agricultural production, railway transport, heating and stationary motors is SKK 4 100 per 1 000 litres.

Spain. For unleaded petrol of more than 97 IO, the rate is EUR 402.92 per 1 000 litres.

Sweden. Unleaded petrol and diesel are divided into environmental classes. For unleaded petrol there are two rates: SEK 4 710 and SEK 4 740. For diesel used in all kinds of motor driven vehicles there are three rates: SEK 3 178, SEK 3 417 and SEK 3 730.

Switzerland. As of 1 January 2000, leaded petrol is no longer sold.

United Kingdom. For domestic purposes (or supplies under 2 300 litres) VAT rate is 5%. The UK market is composed mainly of ultra-low sulphur petrol (ULSP) and ultra low sulphur diesel (ULSD); hence rates for ULSP and ULSD are given rather than for unleaded petrol and conventional diesel.

United States. The weighted average rate of Federal and State taxes in 2003 was USD 0.427 per gallon on petrol (leaded and unleaded) and USD 0.484 for diesel fuel. The Federal rate on petrol (leaded and unleaded) was USD 0.184 per gallon in 2003. 1 US gallon is 3.785 litres. The Federal rate on diesel was USD 0.244 per gallon in 2003. "Gasohol" (mixtures of petrol and alcohol) was taxed at a Federal rate of USD 0.130-0.15436 per gallon in 2003 depending on content of alcohol. There is no Federal VAT.

Source: National Delegates; position as at 1 January 2003.

Table 4.5. **Taxation of tobacco**

	Cigarettes				Cigars[2]				Tax on rolling tobacco for cigarettes			
	Specific excise per 1 000		*Ad valorem* excise	VAT	Specific excise per 1 000		*Ad valorem* excise	VAT	Specific excise per 1 000		*Ad valorem* excise	VAT
	National currency	USD	(% of RSP)[1]	%	National currency	USD	(% of RSP)[1]	%	National currency	USD	(% of RSP)[1]	%
Australia*	215.24	120.86	0.00	10.00	See note		0.00	10.00	269.05	151.07	0.00	10.00
Austria*	21.38	22.45	42.00	20.00	0.00	0.00	13.00	20.00	0.00	0.00	47.00	20.00
Belgium	19. 86	20.86	45.84	21.00	0.00	0.00	5.00	21.00	0.00	0.00	37.55	21.00
Canada*	79.25	50.41	n/a	7 or 15	14.79	9.41	See note	7 or 15	54.00	34.35	n/a	7 or 15
Czech Republic	360.00	12.00	0.00	22.00	360.00	12.00	5.00	22.00	440.00	14.66	5.00	22.00
Denmark*	606.80	85.81	21.22	25.00	198.00	28.00	10.00	25.00	452.50	63.99	0.00	25.00
Finland*	15.13	15.89	50.00	22.00	0.00	0.00	22.00	22.00	3.62	3.80	50.00	22.00
France	7.50	7.88	55.19	19.60	0.00	0.00	20.00	19.60	0.00	0.00	51.69	19.60
Germany	61.70	64.79	24.23	16.00	13.00	13.65	1.00	16.00	21.40	22.47	18.32	16.00
Greece	4.55	4.77	53.86	18.00	0.00	0.00	26.00	18.00	0.00	0.00	59.00	18.00
Hungary	4 200.00	18.73	18.00	25.00	0.00	0.00	25.00	25.00	0.00	0.00	32.00	25.00
Iceland	7 274.00	90.05	47.31	24.50	5 200.00	64.38	44.56	24.50	5 200.00	64.38	44.56	24.50
Ireland	124.94	131.20	18.46	21.00	185.70	195.00	0.00	21.00	156.70	164.55	0.00	21.00
Italy	0.00	0.00	58.00	20.00	0.00	0.00	23.00	20.00	0.00	0.00	54.00	20.00
Japan*	7 072.00	59.56	0.00	5.00	7 072.00	59.56	0.00	5.00	7 072.00	59.56	0.00	5.00
Korea*	38 250.00	32.27	0.00	10.00	78 000.00	65.81	0.00	10.00	27 300.00	23.03	0.00	10.00
Luxembourg	11.89	12.49	45.84	12.00	0.00	0.00	5.00	12.00	0.00	0.00	31.50	12.00
Mexico*	0.00	0.00	80 or 107	15.00	0.00	0.00	20.90	15.00	0.00	0.00	20.90	15.00
Netherlands	53.27	55.94	20.51	19.00	0.00	0.00	5.00	19.00	21.96	23.06	13.69	19.00
New Zealand*	263.41	138.05	0.00	12.50	See note		0.00	12.50	329.27	172.56	0.00	12.50
Norway	1 740.00	251.27	0.00	24.00	1 740.00	251.27	0.00	24.00	1 200.00	173.29	0.00	24.00
Poland	52.00	13.55	25.00	22.00	123.00	32.04	–	22.00	0.00	0.00	60.00	22.00
Portugal*	42.60	44.73	23.00	19.00	0.00	0.00	12.00	19.00	0.00	0.00	36.00	19.00
Slovak Republic*	950.00	24.06	–	20.00	950.00	24.06	–	20.00	1 000.00	25.33	–	20.00
Spain	3.00	3.15	54.00	16.00	0.00	0.00	12.50	16.00	0.00	0.00	37.50	16.00
Sweden	200.00	23.05	39.20	25.00	560.00	64.53	0.00	25.00	630.00	72.60	0.00	25.00
Switzerland*	72.00	52.14	53.75	7.60	2.60/12.10	1.88/8.76	0.00	7.60	1.50/9.00	1.09/6.52	0.00	7.60
Turkey*	1 250 000.00	0.78	55.30	18.00	0.00	0.00	55.30	18.00	0.00	0.00	55.30	18.00
United Kingdom	94.24	151.86	22.00	17.50	137.26	221.18	0.00	17.50	98.66	158.98	0.00	17.50
United States*	See note				See note				See note			

Table 4.5. **Taxation of tobacco** *(cont.)*

1. **RSP.** Retail selling price.
2. **Cigars.** Canada, Denmark and Japan tax cigars at a rate per 1 000 pieces and not according to weight. In Canada and Denmark it is assumed that a cigar weighs 3 grams and in Japan 1 gram.

Australia. The taxation of cigars and cigarettes applies a per stick rate if tobacco content per stick does not exceed 0.8 g. Where the tobacco content exceeds 0.8 g. per stick, the excise duty rate is AUD 269.05 per kg. Excise on snuff is imposed at a rate of AUD 2.19 per kg.

Austria. The excise duty on cigars is 13% of RSP, at least EUR 32.7 for 1 000 pieces.

Canada. An additional excise duty on cigars is applicable at the greater of CAD 65 per 1 000 and 65% computed on the sales price for domestically manufactured cigars or on their duty paid value in the case of imported cigars. Provinces add their own taxes on tobacco products. For cigarettes, these range between CAD 103 and CAD 210 per thousand. Rolling tobacco ranges from CAD 46.80 and CAD 200 per kg. Some provinces also apply an *ad valorem* tax.

Denmark. The excise tax for other smoking tobaccos is DKK 402.5/1 000 g. for coarse-cut tobacco. As of 1 October 2003, the specific excise per 1 000 cigarettes is DKK 489.2 and 21.22% of RSP.

Finland. Cigarette paper: *ad valorem* excise 60% of RSP.

Japan. The tax consists of a national element, a prefectural element and a municipal element. The rate for cigars is JPY 7 072 for 1 000 pieces (same tax as for cigarettes).

Korea. The figures above include local government excise tax and the education tax (50% of the amount of the local government excise tax).

Mexico. The rates are 80 and 107%. The lower rate applies to cheaper cigarettes without filter and with dark tobacco.

New Zealand. The rate shown for cigarettes is the rate of 1 000 pieces not exceeding 0.8 kg in actual tobacco content. Cigarettes exceeding 0.8 kg in actual tobacco content per 1 000 are taxed as cigars. Excise rate for cigars is NZD 329.27 per 1 000 g. of tobacco content of cigars.

Portugal. Excise tax on cigarettes is reduced to EUR 6.10 and 35% for small producers in the Azores and Madeira.

Slovak Republic. Excise rate on other tabacco is SKK 880/1 000 g. and excise rate on snuff and chewing tobacco is SKK 880/1 000 g.

Switzerland. "Specific excise per 1 000 for cigars": the tax between the maximum and minimum depends on the retail selling price per piece and the average weight per 1 000 pieces. "Specific excise per 1 000 g. for rolling tobacco for cigarettes": the tax between the maximum and minimum depends on the retail selling price.

Turkey. The figure for "Specific Excise per 1 000 cigarettes" is for cigarettes whose retail sales price is up to and including TRL 1 600 000. For cigarettes whose retail sales price is between TRL 1 600 001 and TRL 3 050 000, the Specific Excise per 1 000 is TRL 2 500 000, or USD 1.55. For cigarettes whose retail sales price is TRL 3 050 001 and over, the Specific Excise per 1 000 is TRL 4 000 000, or USD 2.48.

United States. State taxes vary widely. The weighted average of Federal and State taxes on a pack of cigarettes was USD 0.87 in 2002. Payments under the 1998 Master Settlement Agreement between tobacco companies and the individual States have been estimated to add another USD 0.45 per pack. In 2003, Federal specific excise tax rates on tobacco were: USD 19.50 per thousand for small cigarettes (no more than 3 pounds per thousand); USD 40.95 per thousand for large cigarettes; USD 1.828 per thousand for small cigars weighing no more than 3 pounds per thousand; 20.719% of the manufacturers price but not more than USD 48.75 per thousand for large cigars; USD 0.0122 per 50 papers for cigarette paper; USD 0.585 per pound for snuff; USD 0.195 per pound for chewing tobacco; USD 1.0969 per pound for pipe tobacco and for roll-your-own tobacco. There is no Federal VAT.

Source: National Delegates; position as at 1 January 2003.

ISBN 92-64-00676-1
Consumption Tax Trends
VAT/GST and Excise Rates, Trends and Administration Issues

Chapter 5

Taxing Vehicles

Principles

Vehicle taxation in its widest definition represents a prime example of the use of the whole spectrum of consumption taxes. Taxes levied on motor vehicles may broadly be divided into two categories: taxes on the acquisition or registration of motor vehicles and taxes on their use.

Taxes on the acquisition of motor vehicles may include once and for all payments of VAT (Table 5.1) or excise duties (Table 5.2) or other fees and charges associated with the registration of a vehicle. These taxes may vary considerably from one country to another. VAT is normally calculated on the basis of the retail-selling price including excise duties. VAT on used vehicles may be applied to the full selling price or only in respect of the margin between the buying and the selling price.

Taxes on the use of vehicles include recurring charges levied on the right to drive on public roads (also called taxes on ownership), usually in the form of an annual motor tax. Taxes on the operation of motor vehicles that include excise duties on fuel and motorway charges or other road user tolls. Table 4.4 gives an overview of the taxation of motor fuel, the most significant tax related to the operation of motor vehicles.

In addition, many of these charges will incur VAT or sales tax which in most cases will be levied on the final duty paid value. VAT or sales tax will also apply to general maintenance and running costs.

Recurring taxes on the ownership of motor vehicles can also take many forms. The main elements used to assess these kinds of taxes are weight, usage and vehicle type, type of fuel and engine size. Other specific criteria are also used.

According to the circumstances, motor vehicles may be taxed either in the country of registration or in the country where they are operating. Acquisition and recurring ownership taxes normally apply in the country of registration and taxes on fuels and road user charges apply where the vehicle is operating. A haulier from a country with high registration and/or ownership taxes may be commercially disadvantaged by also having to pay high fuel taxes and tolls for the circulation of its vehicles in countries where ownership charges are low. The question is how to balance these two factors.

However, unlike many other products, the differences in the taxation of motor vehicles in general do not give rise to cross border shopping as motor vehicles need to be registered in the principal country of use with a unique identification number. Even in the integrated market of the European Union there has been no harmonisation or even approximation of taxes or tax rates on motor vehicles (except for minimum EU motor vehicles tax rates in respect of heavy lorries and the ending of the increased VAT rate). While a resident of an EU member State may buy a vehicle anywhere in the EU, the vehicle remains liable to be registered in the country of residence of the person acquiring the vehicle and the relevant taxes are, in principle, levied in that country.

Links with other policy areas

Whilst taxation of motor vehicles is a significant source of revenue for most countries, fiscal policy considerations must take due account of equally important issues involving other policy areas in the field of transport, energy and environment. Transport (and general trade) policy may require that the total tax burden on heavy goods vehicles is kept reasonably low to help stimulate commercial activity, or taxation of motor vehicles could be designed to move transport from road to rail or from private to public transport. Energy and environmental policies may require high taxation of motor vehicles as a means of controlling consumer behaviour to conserve energy and reduce pollution.

In general terms, very high taxes are likely to limit the number of motor vehicles on the road. However, while this would at first appear to favour environmental policy, higher taxes on the acquisition of new motor cars invariably means that there is a greater population of old cars polluting the atmosphere. To combat this some countries have introduced short term bonus schemes to scrap old cars and encourage the purchase of new cars.

One of the most popular examples of using a fiscal instrument for common policy purposes is the differentiation between various qualities of fuel. When unleaded petrol was introduced onto the market the pump price of the product was not competitive with the less environmentally friendly leaded product (added to this was the fact that the number of cars with catalytic converters, which required unleaded petrol, was low in many countries.). The solution to the problem was a tax differentiation between leaded and unleaded petrol to make unleaded petrol retail prices significantly cheaper and thus more attractive to the consumer. The result is that leaded petrol now has virtually disappeared from the market in most OECD countries (partly due to the tax rate differences, partly due to regulations).

Nevertheless, Table 4.4 shows that large differences remain in the tax rates applicable in the member countries, especially as concerns unleaded petrol and light fuel oil. The difference in the tax levels for petrol and diesel in European and North American member countries remains particularly striking.

Table 5.1. **VAT on sale and registration of motor vehicles**

	Sale or import*	Registration	Limitations for the deduction of input tax	Exemptions	Reduced Rates	Preferences of low-emission vehicles
Australia	Yes	No	Yes[1]	Yes[2]	No	No
Austria	Yes	No	Yes	Yes	No	No
Belgium	Yes	No	Yes[3]	No[4]	No	No
Canada	Yes	No[5]	Yes[6]	No[7]	No	No
Czech Republic	No	No	No	No	No	No
Denmark	Yes	No	No	Yes	No	No
Finland	Yes	No	Yes[8]	No	No	No
France	Yes	No	Yes[9]	No	No	No
Germany	Yes	No	No	No	No	No
Greece	Yes	Yes	Yes	No	No	No
Hungary[10]	Yes	Yes	Yes	No	No	No
Iceland	Yes	No	Yes	No	No	No
Ireland	Yes	No	Yes	No	No	No
Italy	Yes	No	Yes	No	No	No
Japan	Yes	No	No	Yes[11]	No	No
Korea	Yes	No	Yes[12]	No	No	No
Luxembourg	Yes	No	No	Yes	No	No
Mexico	Yes	No	No	No	Yes[13]	No
Netherlands	Yes	No	Yes[14]	No	No	No
New Zealand	Yes	Yes	No	No	No	No
Norway	Yes	No	Yes	No[15]	No	Yes[15]
Poland	Yes	No	Yes	No	No	No
Portugal	Yes	No	Yes	No	No	No
Slovak Republic	Yes	No	Yes	No	No	No
Spain	Yes	No	Yes	No	Yes	No
Sweden	Yes	No	Yes	No	No	No
Switzerland[16]	Yes	No	Yes	Yes	No	No
Turkey	Yes	No	Yes	No	Yes	No
United Kingdom	Yes	No	Yes	Yes	No	No
United States	No	No	No	No	No	No

* Sale or import: in the EU most goods are charged with VAT in the country in which they are purchased by private individuals (or business or legal entity which is not registrable for VAT). However, for a new vehicle, boat or aircraft, VAT will be due in the member State of destination (registration).

1. Limitations may apply to purchases of second hand vehicles from unregistered entities.
2. Cars for use by people with disabilities may be purchased GST-free (that is, these purchases are zero-rated).
3. The right of deduction with respect to VAT incurred on the purchase of or on expenses relating to passenger cars (including those which are used also for the transport of goods) can not be higher than 50%.
4. However, cars for the handicapped are zero-rated.
5. Persons who purchase motor vehicles from GS/HST registrants in a non-participating province or outside Canada are required to pay the provincial component (8%) of the Harmonized Sales Tax when the vehicle is registered in a participating province.
6. Generally, the amount of the input tax credit that may be claimed is based on the percentage of use in commercial activities (in some cases, if use is 50% or less, there is no input tax credit). However, in the case of an individual or a partnership, the amount of the input tax credit is generally based on the capital cost allowance (CCA) claimed for income tax purposes.
7. The sale of a vehicle by an individual otherwise than in the course of a commercial activity is not subject to GST/HST.
8. Finnish VAT law does not permit deductions where the acquisition concerns passenger cars. However, this restriction does not apply to vehicles acquired to be sold, leased or used for commercial passenger transport or by driving schools or to cars acquired exclusively for a purpose that gives the right to deduct. The restriction of the right to deduct also applies to goods and services related to cars and their use.
9. VAT is not deductible on the acquisition of multipurpose passenger motor vehicles, or on any related service, if these vehicles are used as fixed assets, or, if that is not the case, are not intended for resale. However, this exclusion does not applyto the following:
   - vehicles acquired by public transport companies used exclusively for the public transport of passengers;
   - road vehicles seating more than eight passengers, not including the driver, used by companies to transport their staff in connection with their work;
   - hired vehicles, provided that the hire is subject to VAT;
   - vehicles used exclusively for driver training.
10. In the case of new means of transport, VAT (plus registration tax as of 1 February 2004) is paid at registration.
11. Vehicles for the physically handicapped are exempt from taxation.
12. The non-business use of the small vehicle has limitations for the deduction of input tax.
13. In the border region a reduced VAT rate of 10% is applicable both for industries and individuals.
14. For private use.
15. Sales of vehicles that exclusively use electricity for propulsion are zero-rated.
16. VAT levied because of the use: for instance, on fuel, oil and repairs including spare parts. Limitations for the deduction of input tax: private use or use for exempt purposes of the vehicle. VAT exemptions: transport of sick, injured or disabled people in vehicles specially equipped for this purpose.

Table 5.2. **Excise on sale and registration of motor vehicles**

	Sale	Registration	Exemptions	Reduced rates	Preferences of low-emission vehicles
Australia	Yes[1]	No	Yes[2]	No	No
Austria	Yes	Yes	Yes	No	Yes
Belgium	No	No	n/a	n/a	n/a
Canada	Yes[3]	No	Yes[4]	No	No
Czech Republic	No	No	No	No	No
Denmark	No	Yes	Yes	Yes	Yes
Finland	No	Yes	Yes	Yes	No
France	No	Yes[5]	Yes[6]	Yes[7]	Yes[8]
Germany	No	No	Yes	No	Yes
Greece	Yes	Yes	Yes	Yes	Yes
Hungary	No	No	No	No	No
Iceland	Yes	No	Yes	No	No
Ireland	No	Yes	Yes	No	Yes
Italy	No	No	No	No	No
Japan	Yes	No	Yes	Yes	Yes
Korea	Yes	No	Yes[9]	No	No
Luxembourg	No	No	Yes	No	No
Mexico	Yes	No	Yes	No	No
Netherlands	No	No	No	No	No
New Zealand	No	No	No	No	No
Norway	No[10]	Yes	Yes	Yes	Yes
Poland	Yes[11]				
Portugal	No	Yes[12]	Yes	No	No
Slovak Republic	No	No	No	No	No
Spain	No	Yes	Yes	Yes	No
Sweden	No	No	No	Yes	No
Switzerland	Yes[13]	Yes[14]	Yes[15]	Yes[16]	Yes[17]
Turkey	Yes[18]	No	Yes	No	No
United Kingdom	No	No	Yes	Yes	Yes
United States	Yes	Yes	Yes	Yes	Yes

1. Luxury Car Tax is applied to the sale of new passenger vehicles (designed to carry less than two tonnes and fewer than nine passengers and all limousines, regardless of their capacity) as 25 per cent of the value in excess of AUD 57 009 of the vehicle.
2. Exemptions exist for emergency vehicles, vehicles fitted out for transporting the disabled and commercial vehicles not designed for carrying passengers.
3. Excise taxes levied on automotive air conditioners and heavy cars.
4. Diplomats and Foreign Armed Services excluded.
5. Tax on registration certificates.
6. New vehicles sold by agents and dealers of specific makes of cars in show rooms.
7. Lorries with gross weight of over 3.5 tons.
8. Under certain conditions, for vehicles which run on electricity, natural gas or LPG.
9. There are excise exemptions for the handicapped.
10. However, a special re-registration tax applies for domestic sales of cars.
11. Excise duty rates for: *a)* sale of passenger cars effected prior to their first registration: 12% for passenger cars with engine capacity over 2 000 cm^2; 3% for others; *b)* passenger car imports effected within two calendar years of their production: 13.6% for passenger cars with engine capacity over 2 000 cm^2; 3.1% for others. (The difference in the level of percentage excise duty rates on domestic cars and imported cars results solely from the difference in the taxable base, adopted for excise tax calculation purposes.) In the case of the sale and importation of passenger cars effected after two calendar years from the date of manufacture, the excise duty rates are calculated according to a formula. Increased excise tax rates for old passenger cars are applicable to both imported cars and cars sold in the country prior to their first registration. (A new excise duty scheme for the taxation of passenger cars will enter into force fully as from 1 May 2004.)
12. The "Imposto Automovel" (Motor car tax) is an excise whose scope is the license plate registration of new or used cars, imported into or manufactured in Portugal.
13. Import taxes (no cars produced in Switzerland).
14. Fees for the number plates and registration papers.
15. Disabled people.
16. Famers and foresters.
17. Electro-cars.
18. Special Consumption Tax is meant as Excise.

ISBN 92-64-00676-1
Consumption Tax Trends
VAT/GST and Excise Rates, Trends and Administration Issues

Chapter 6

Globalisation of Services and Intangibles: The Consumption Tax Challenge

The spread of value added taxes around the world has coincided with a rapid growth in the value of the international trade in services and intangibles. Since 1997, service exports have been growing across the OECD countries at 3.3% per year on average whilst service imports have grown by 4.1% per year. Goods still remain the major item of international trade for OECD countries but in 2002 services accounted for 21.9% of total exports of goods and services and 20.5% of total imports of goods and services. This growth has been fuelled by a number of factors, including deregulation, privatisation, technology and the globalisation.

In 2003, the OECD's Consumption Tax Technical Advisory Group (a group that had been formed to assist in the development of the OECD's work on taxation of electronic commerce, comprising representatives from OECD and non-OECD governments and from business) published a report that drew attention to a number of issues concerning the application of consumption taxes to internationally traded services and intangibles. It pointed out that a number of the issues that were causing problems for electronically traded services were also problems for conventionally traded services. As the international trade in the sector has grown, so the difficulties caused by these taxes have become more apparent.

The OECD has since taken a closer look at these issues and has found a number of symptoms such as double taxation, unintentional double non-taxation, and disincentives for businesses to enter new markets. These symptoms frequently come about through differing approaches to taxing services, differing interpretations and definitions and uncertainty. Most countries try to relieve exports of services from tax whilst levying tax on imported services, thus drawing a parallel with the treatment of goods. However, the intangible nature of many internationally traded services is such that the ease with which this fundamental approach can be applied to goods does not always apply to services.

Most OECD countries try to tax consumption of services and intangibles where it takes place. The European Union tries to achieve this, in general, by the Place of Supply of Services rules (Article 9 of the Sixth VAT Directive). These were written in 1977 and provide a basic rule that the place of supply of a service is where the supplier is established. This achieves (or, perhaps, "achieved" might be more accurate) the "consumption" test because in 1977 most services were consumed in the country in which they were delivered. Over the years the EU has made many exceptions to this rule in order to meet the principle of taxing "where consumed", reflecting the growth in international trade. The latest of these exceptions was that relating to the supply of electronic services, a change that came into effect in July 2003. This legislative approach demands that services are very specifically defined in order to provide legal and administrative certainty, otherwise the basic rule (tax where the supplier is established) will apply. An example of this was the European Court of Justice ruling in the case of von Hoffmann (C-145/96, *Bernd von Hoffmann v. Finanzamt Trier*). This case turned on an interpretation of the meaning of "services of … lawyers … and other similar services" and whether this applied to the service of a professional arbitrator. In an outcome that surprised many the Court ruled that an arbitrator's services are not "similar" to a lawyer's services and, as a result arbitrators supplying their services to their clients (both inside and outside the European Union) should add Valued Added Tax to their accounts, whilst non-EU arbitrators can enjoy providing tax-free services to their EU clients.

A further disadvantage of the EU's approach may be an inherent lack of flexibility to react to emerging market changes. Twice in recent years, the EU has had to act in order to protect its own industries, firstly with the telecommunications industry in 1997 and secondly with the electronic commerce sector in 2003. But on both occasions much revenue had been lost by EU governments before the changes could be implemented. Many EU companies had suffered significant competitive distortion in that they had to account for VAT on their domestic sales in a market in which non-EU suppliers could make supplies to the same customers without VAT. In the case of electronic commerce, US companies, especially Internet service providers (ISPs), are still probably running with the advantages of being first in the marketplace even if they now have to account for VAT. Even though their customers now have to pay the tax how many are prepared to change their ISP, something that means changing long-established e-mail addresses?

Some other OECD countries, mainly those that have adopted a value added tax in the last 15 years or so, have taken a different approach in that they simply tax a service if it is consumed in their country. This, in most cases, means that it is not necessary to define the service to the extent necessary under European law, but it does mean that "consumption" has to be defined. This can be done through the use of proxies such as establishment or residence (sometimes described as "connected with real property"), or physical performance. Thus, although this is a significantly different approach it tries to achieve the same result as in the EU member States. Therefore, if an arbitrator based in Australia provided services to a client based in New Zealand the question of taxation would depend on how consumption was characterised in the circumstances (rather than a precise definition of the service provided). It is likely that as the New Zealand client was receiving the arbitrator's verdict then both countries would regard that as a service "consumed" in New Zealand and no Australian tax would apply but New Zealand would require taxation.

A growing issue for all countries using value added taxes is that of the treatment of "management services". Typically, this is a mechanism used by related businesses as a means of ensuring that a subsidiary company is charged with overheads provided by the holding company. This ensures that the subsidiary's profits are not artificially high as a result of many of its overhead costs being absorbed by the holding company. But "management services" may also be little more than a means of moving profits from one country to another, possibly for income tax reasons. As globalisation continues, this is a key issue for both tax administrations and for international businesses. In the European Union, defining "management services" in order to determine the place of supply can be particularly difficult and probably has to be done on a case by case basis. Equally, for those countries that apply place of taxation on the basis of "consumption" or "performance" defining where "management services" are performed can be equally difficult.

Clearly the scope for getting it "wrong" is quite high. If countries interpret a definition of a service differently, or they characterise "consumption" or "performance" in different ways then the symmetry between taxed imports and non-taxed exports is at risk. The result is either double taxation or double non-taxation. In many cases, even though this may not be end result, the inherent uncertainties mean that businesses frequently have to seek clarification from their tax advisers or from the relevant tax authorities before undertaking transactions. Indeed they may even be discouraged from developing new markets precisely because of the consumption tax uncertainties.

Other causes of problems include lack of internationally agreed approaches to refunding value added taxes to non-resident businesses. A small number of OECD countries allow a non-resident business to register even though the company makes no taxable supplies there. This enables companies that incur tax on expenses in that country to recover the tax, subject to necessary safeguards to protect the tax authority from fraud. Other countries may allow non-resident businesses to submit special claims, again subject to anti-fraud safeguards. However, whilst some countries will allow refunds to non-residents of any country others are prepared to grant refunds only if the business is resident in a country that provides refunds on a reciprocal basis.

In tackling these issues, the OECD recognises that there cannot be a "harmonised" system that every country will apply. Sovereignty in tax matters is such that this would not be a reasonable approach, nor would it be practical in terms of achievement. However, the OECD does feel that some basic principles to apply to the taxation of cross-border services and intangibles should be agreed by its member countries and that these principles should help form the basis of a commonly understood position. In developing these principles it might be useful to bear in mind some basic principles that apply to value added taxes. Firstly, these taxes are taxes on consumption. Businesses act as (unpaid) tax collectors throughout the supply chain but the intention is that as long as they make taxable supplies they should be able to run their businesses without incurring tax as a cost. There are some exceptions to this of course, primarily in the exempt sector where insurance and financial services are treated differently. But for most businesses, value added taxes should not be a tax cost.

As a basic rule, a transaction should be taxed only once. Thus, if a supply crosses international borders only one country should be able to apply tax to that transaction. In trying to achieve this goal there will, inevitably, be difficulties and businesses may find themselves caught between two countries, both of whom are determined to levy tax because of their own rules. Clearly this is not an acceptable situation and would not happen within a domestic market so should not happen internationally. It may be that the OECD can provide for some sort of model agreement between countries on how to resolve these issues and it may also be possible to consider what actions might be possible through dispute resolution mechanisms. Longer term, such agreements may also be necessary to cover supplies of goods where these involve more complex arrangements than simple imports and exports.

The OECD will be working in this area over the period 2004-2006. This will be highly important given the spread of value added taxes and the growth in internationally traded services and intangibles. As trade between the world's regions continues to grow the current problems will not go away and are likely to get worse rather than better. At present there is too much uncertainty, too much double taxation and too much unintentional non-taxation. All of this leads to a brake being applied to developing trade and general economic growth and whilst there will be no easy answers the challenge will be to minimise both the obstacles and the uncertainties.

ISBN 92-64-00676-1
Consumption Tax Trends
VAT/GST and Excise Rates, trends and Administration Issues

Chapter 7

Financial Services – Emerging Approaches to a Perennial Problem

The application of value added taxes to the financial services sector has long been problematic. Most value added taxes apply to supplies of goods and services whereas supplies of money (including banknotes and negotiable instruments) are rarely classified as either. Further, there are problems regarding valuation. With "normal" supplies of goods and services there is usually a clear value on which the tax may be applied. But valuation of financial instruments and ways of characterising financial services make application much more difficult. How, for instance, to measure the value of a life assurance policy? Should it be on the premiums payable during the term of the policy or on the terminal value of the policy? Should the interest charged on goods sold on credit be subject to tax, thus making credit purchases even more expensive? Should the interest earned on deposits by private individuals be subject to tax? Indeed, can interest even be classified as a supply for value added tax purposes?

Studies by both academics and governments have been carried out over the years but to date there has been little actual movement away from the original "solution" to the problem – that of granting exemption to a wide range of such services (in some OECD countries this is referred as "input taxing"). However, these exemptions do undermine the central premise of neutrality of value added tax, *i.e.* that it is a tax on consumption by consumers rather than a tax on business. Business should collect the tax on behalf of the consumers through the multi-stage process but it should not be borne by business as a tax cost.

Exemption for banks and others in the supply chain means that significant amounts of input tax on goods and services acquired by the financial service sector are irrecoverable. Thus in calculating their charges to customers the sector will factor in this "embedded" tax, which will then cascade through the supply chain. The result of this is that the effective tax rate on goods and services paid for by consumers is higher than the actual tax rate. Indeed, some countries, especially those with large financial service sectors, rely on the input tax blocked as a result of exemption for a significant element of their total value added tax revenue. In the United Kingdom one estimate (McCormick K. (2003), in *Cahiers de droit fiscal international – Consumption Taxation and Financial Services, Volume LXXXVIIIb*, International Fiscal Association, Rotterdam, pp. 757-780) is that the irrecoverable VAT incurred by the banking and insurance sectors alone come to the equivalent of around EUR 4.5 billion, or roughly 4.7% of the net receipts of the tax.

Exemption also raises obstacles to outsourcing business activities. Businesses are increasingly buying in services that were previously performed in-house, thus allowing the business to concentrate on its core functions. For the financial services sector value added taxes become a real cost as any supplier of such services will normally have to add tax to the price of the services supplied, whereas performing the service in-house means there is no value added tax cost. The inability to recover this tax means that exemption, and the associated inability to deduct all the input tax incurred, may well reduce, or even nullify, the reduced costs that outsourcing often delivers.

Not only does the exemption approach raise policy concerns but it also leads to compliance and administrative costs for the financial services sector and for tax administrations. Most financial service suppliers do have some taxable outputs, possibly in respect of exported financial services which are usually exempt with refund – more often referred to as "zero-rated" – or because they make domestic supplies that do not fall within the exempt category. As a result they are entitled to some recovery of input tax and this often leads to complex methodologies being adopted in order to maximise the recovery rate. At its simplest this can be achieved by:

- blocking input tax recovery on those inputs directly attributable to exempt supplies;
- allowing total recovery of input tax incurred on inputs directly attributable to taxable suppliers; and
- allowing partial recovery on input tax incurred on inputs that cannot be directly attributable to either exempt or taxable supplies.

Other, more sophisticated, methodologies are often adopted, but all lead to complex calculations and, not infrequently, to disputes between administrations and taxpayers. Aggressive tax planning may also be encouraged in order to maximise recovery rates.

New approaches

Recent years have seen some evidence that countries are beginning to rethink the treatment of the sector. Australia, when it adopted its Goods and Services Tax (GST) in July 2000, recognised the disincentive that exemption creates for outsourcing and introduced the Reduced Input Tax Credit scheme (RITC). This allows a fixed recovery rate (currently 75%) in respect of input tax incurred on the activities that are most frequently outsourced. Although this doesn't remove the issue of breaching the central tenet of value added tax (that of placing the tax burden on consumers rather than businesses) it does help with the disincentive to outsource activities. However, even with this facility the complexities of attributing input tax to specific outputs, and determining a recovery rate for unattributable input tax, are still present. The compliance costs are often quite high, although it is arguable that the sector may prefer these higher compliance costs when outweighed by higher input tax recovery.

In 2003 the European Commission indicated that it intended to review the rules in the Sixth VAT Directive on VAT and financial services. The 6th Directive governs most of the ways in which VAT applies in the European Union and Article 13 includes the rules for applying VAT to financial services, including definitions of what falls to be exempt. These rules were agreed in 1977 although in some cases their provenance is even older and the sector has changed dramatically in the years since. New financial instruments and cross-border dealing have changed the face and nature of financial services and, as a result, there have been many cases heard by the courts, including the European Court of Justice (ECJ), on the interpretation of the Article 13 definitions. However, the Commission's review is not intended to propose any significant departure from the fundamental approach of exemption for the financial service sector, but rather it will limit itself to a significant update of the definitions of exempt services.

As banks and other financial service suppliers have increasingly outsourced their back-office operations in recent years this question of definition has become vital. If a service is outsourced then does it retain its exemption by still falling under the exemption definition or is it so far removed from the actual financial supply that it is no longer identifiable as an exempt financial service? This was addressed by the ECJ in the *Sparekassernes Datacenter* (SDC) case (C-2/95) in which the Court ruled that transactions are exempted "according to the nature of the services provided and not according to the person supplying or receiving the services". In that case the Court's view was that the supplies at issue were still sufficiently connected to the transfers of funds that they were able to retain their exempt status. But this will not always be the case and the application of tax to an outsourced activity may well be sufficient to discourage the financial service company from achieving the savings that would otherwise accrue through outsourcing. Within the EU, the growth of cross border banking structures has caused additional strain in this area.

New Zealand has undertaken the most radical steps in its recent change to the way in which it treats financial services. Put simply they have legislated for zero-rating (*i.e.* exemption with refund) financial services when services are supplied to a customer whose outputs are at least 75% taxable. Thus a bank providing financial services to a manufacturer or retailer whose outputs are taxable can recover the input tax incurred in respect of these supplies. This leads to a significantly higher overall recovery rate of input tax. However, a bank providing financial services to another exempt financial services company or to a consumer would still be unable to recover input tax (other than to the extent that it could do so under the old rules).

Whilst this is a significant step towards removing the "embedded tax" problem that damages the neutrality principle it does, of course, come with a significant tax cost to the New Zealand Government. Interestingly it was introduced at the same time that New Zealand also brought in provisions to impose a reverse charge on imported services so there was an element of *quid pro quo*. For many countries (including the United Kingdom which, as noted above, collects a significant amount of VAT revenue from blocking input tax recovery in the sector) the fiscal effects of such a step would be such that an upward adjustment in tax rates would probably be necessary in order to make good the tax foregone.

Outside the OECD it is interesting to note that South Africa, which introduced an EU model VAT in 1991, reviewed the financial services treatment a few years later and, as a result, imposed VAT at the standard rate on a range of explicit fee-based services that had previously been exempt. The resulting trends have been for financial service providers to move more towards taxable fee-based services as most of their customers are likely to be taxable businesses with the ability to recover all input tax and, of course, the financial service sector increases its input tax recoverability rate under partial exemption methodologies. Again, beyond the OECD, Singapore has applied a mix of the Australian and New Zealand approaches, allowing suppliers of financial services to treat exempt supplies as taxable when supplied to taxable persons. They go on to provide simplified mechanisms for determining the recovery rate of input tax.

Other solutions to the problem have been considered. In the 1990s a series of reports for the European Commission by Ernst and Young outlined and proposed a truncated cash flow method VAT. Put very simply, cash inflows from financial transactions are considered as outputs and cash outflows are regarded as inputs. However, whilst this might well go a long way to removing the lack of neutrality problem it does raise other issues, including disclosure of bank profit margins to customers. Although this demonstrated that it was in principle possible to apply VAT to financial services, the resultant complexity was felt to be a major disadvantage. There is no evidence that OECD countries have attempted to legislate along these lines. Outside the OECD some countries, *e.g.* Israel and Argentina, apply VAT on gross interest but these do not always remove cascading problems and bring their own complications to administration.

In the years ahead it seems likely that policy-makers and academics will continue to examine ways in which financial services can be better treated, especially with the intention of reducing the cascade effect of limiting input tax deduction. Countries with either a very low VAT rate or a comparatively small financial service economy may well be able to develop some new thinking and put that into practice. However, for those countries with higher rates and with large financial service sectors it seems that the effects of any radical change would probably have a significant impact on revenue collection. Perhaps for those countries the best that can be achieved is a simplification of the rules governing input tax recovery.

ISBN 92-64-00676-1
Consumption Tax Trends
VAT/GST and Excise Rates, trends and Administration Issues

Chapter 8

Reducing VAT Revenue Leakage: Improved Approaches are Needed in Many Countries

Introduction

Recent years have witnessed a growth in attacks on the systems of value added taxes in many OECD member countries and beyond. Within the European Union (EU), major concerns have been expressed at the incidence of VAT revenue leakage, and the associated practices that have led to these losses. More broadly, many countries have acknowledged that they are suffering from systemic attacks, leading to significant losses of revenue and, in some cases, adverse media coverage. Against this worrying trend, the OECD's Committee on Fiscal Affairs has undertaken work with member countries to ascertain the extent of this non-compliance and the measures being taken to counteract it.

Main abuses encountered

Country reports on the abuses being experienced reflected a large variety of non-compliant behaviour, including: 1) missing trader fraud schemes (sometimes called "carousel" fraud; 2) false/fraudulent/stolen entity registrations or identities to claim false input tax credits, frequently accompanied by the subsequent disappearance of the entity (so-called "phoenix" companies); 3) suppression of reported sales and/or under-valuing/ false invoicing; 4) car "flipping" – automobiles pass through a series of transactions designed to generate profit not from sale, but from GST refunds and rebates, or from non-remitted taxes, often involving non-existent cars and fictitious exports/ sales; 5) various examples involving false exports to claim refunds of input tax credits; 6) asset "flipping", a generalised form of car flipping, and often involving goods such as heavy machinery, cell phones or computer chips; 7) abuses based on arbitrage of cash and accruals accounting methods and differential lodgement periods; 8) artificial tax planning/avoidance schemes; and 9) simple non-registration, non-filing, and non-payment of debts.

Estimates of overall VAT revenue leakage

Estimates of the likely overall revenue losses from VAT non-compliance within member countries are difficult to quantify, for a variety of reasons (*e.g.* gaps in the national measurement of VAT-taxable expenditure, difficulties associated with estimating the impact of exemptions and thresholds, etc., timing considerations). Inquiries across OECD member countries revealed that only one revenue body – the UK Customs and Excise – has a systematic and transparent strategy for measuring overall VAT revenue losses, which is carried out as part of its "Strategic Approach" to tax compliance management. For 2002-03, Customs concluded that around 15.7% of the theoretical VAT tax base for the UK was not collected. During 2004, Customs reported indications of improved compliance, based on a decline in detected missing trader fraud cases and significantly above-budget revenue collections. (Copies of the documents describing the UK Customs and Excise's strategic approach, including its measurement strategy, can be found on the Customs and Excise Web site *www.treasury.gov.uk*.)

Elsewhere, reports of the European Commission have noted various estimates of aggregate revenue losses made in different quarters – a report in 2000 noted that the Court of Auditors had estimated a gap (for 1997) in the region of EUR 70 billion (representing non-compliance of around 17.5%; a report in 2004 noted that some countries have estimated such losses "as up to 10% of net VAT receipts". While it is impossible to be precise, all indications are that the so called VAT gap more than likely exceeds 10% in many EU countries, representing a substantial annual loss to government revenues. While no revenue body can ensure full compliance with the laws, and thereby the collection of all tax revenue, non-compliance in excess of 10% clearly reflects a serious level of non-compliance. For some other OECD countries, revenue leakage does not appear to be a problem of the same magnitude, with "unofficial" reports putting it at no more than a probable 4-6% of the total estimated VAT base.

Countermeasures to reduce incidence of revenue leakage

Based on reports received, OECD member countries have launched a great array of initiatives to address VAT revenue leakage. The main ones identified by OECD members are:

Policy

- The introduction of legislation to create joint and several liability within the supply chain of specified goods such as computers and mobile telephones.
- The introduction of the reverse charge procedure within the construction industry.

Administration

- Considerably enhanced VAT registration processes – "detection is easier than cure" – aimed at the detection and deterrence of fraudulent registrations.
- Earlier detection and investigation of suspect registration/refund claims through use of dedicated audit staff (before the claims are finalised).
- Very early targeting of new businesses for education/service interventions to get these taxpayers on a good compliance path early in their business lifecycle.
- Strengthening of third-party linkages in order to optimise use of available information to verify taxpayers' compliance.
- Targeting specialist staff at criminal elements responsible for attacks on the VAT base.
- Automated cross checking/linkages between income tax and VAT data and records to detect non-compliance situations
- Efforts to improve the quality of business books and records.
- New information reporting regimes.
- Increased penalties and sanctions.
- Additional allocations of resources to increase enforcement efforts in this area.

International co-operation

- Improved sharing of information within groups of countries (*e.g.* the European Union), including the introduction of cross-border audits.
- The introduction of the Secure Exchange of Consumption Tax Information System (SECTIS) within the OECD to exchange information on generic fraud and avoidance developments.

As noted above, the UK has a well documented, transparent, and systematic approach to the identification, assessment, and treatment of VAT compliance risks. In addition to efforts to estimate the extent of the overall and major categories of revenue losses, this strategic approach also provides for a broad range of policy, administrative, and co-operative measures. Implemented over the last few years, this strategic approach appeared to be producing results by mid-2004 with reported increases (over budget) in overall tax revenues and reductions in the incidence of the major categories of tax fraud. This strategic approach is being applied in a number of other countries, at varying levels of intensity.

A need to strengthen the overall management of tax compliance risks

While the measures employed to counteract VAT non-compliance can be expected to have positive benefits, a crucial and ongoing issue for all revenue bodies is the need to systematically assess all compliance risks and ensure that comprehensive measures are in place to address each of the major risks identified. This is by no means a simple and straightforward task, given the large number of risks to be addressed.

In late-2004, the CFA approved a guidance note – Managing and Improving Tax Compliance – that is intended to provide assistance in this regard (the guidance notes are available on *www.oecd.org/ctp/taxguidanceseries*). The guidance note provides a step by step description of a strategic process for the systematic identification, assessment, and treatment of tax compliance risks, and associated monitoring and evaluation activities that are required to gauge the effectiveness of the treatment strategies implemented. In addition to describing the basic principles of risk management in a tax compliance context, the guidance note includes many practical examples drawn from revenue authorities in member countries to illustrate particular approaches and their impacts. It has been derived from a review of the practices of national tax authorities in a number of OECD countries and generally represents the consensus of opinion among expert officials of an effective process for managing tax compliance risks. It is broadly in accord with models of risk management observed in management literature.

The guidance provided on compliance risk management is complemented by two catalogues that provide valuable information from countries' own research efforts and experiences with a variety of compliance strategies.

While the effort and resources needed to employ a strategic approach to compliance risk management are indeed demanding, the experience of UK Customs and Excise over the last few years demonstrates that substantial rewards in terms of improved compliance and associated revenue can be achieved from a comprehensive and sustained risk management approach.

CONSUMPTION TAX TRENDS – ISBN 92-64-00676-1 – © OECD 2005

ISBN 92-64-00676-1
Consumption Tax Trends
VAT/GST and Excise Rates, Trends and Administration Issues

ANNEX 1

Table of exchange rates

As at 1 January 2003

Australia	AUD	1.783
Austria	EUR	0.953
Belgium	EUR	0.953
Canada	CAD	1.573
Czech Republic	CZK	30.113
Denmark	DKK	7.076
Finland	EUR	0.953
France	EUR	0.953
Germany	EUR	0.953
Greece	EUR	0.953
Hungary	HUF	225.030
Iceland	ISK	80.891
Ireland	EUR	0.953
Italy	EUR	0.953
Japan	JPY	118.800
Korea	KRW	1 186.100
Luxembourg	EUR	0.953
Mexico	MXN	10.399
Netherlands	EUR	0.953
New Zealand	NZD	1.910
Norway	NOK	6.928
Poland	PLN	3.839
Portugal	EUR	0.953
Slovak Republic	SKK	39.577
Spain	EUR	0.953
Sweden	SEK	8.684
Switzerland	CHF	1.382
Turkey	TRL	1 669 000.000
United Kingdom	GBP	0.621
United States	USD	1.000

ANNEX 2

Guidelines on E-commerce and Consumption Tax Guidance Series

Since the 1990s, globalisation, deregulation, and technology have all combined to create enormous changes in the volume and pattern of international trade. These changes have in particular stimulated the trade in services and intangibles. Clients, including consumers, now have access to a wide range of products and services offered by business established outside their country of residence. Businesses with multi-national presence may specialize in grouping certain functions in one particular jurisdiction or use shared service centres. As a result the international trade in services and intangibles is growing rapidly, becomes more complex and forms a significant and increasing part of international trade.

This evolution is highly challenging for the management of consumption taxes. The OECD reacted promptly to this situation and, in 1998, adopted the Taxation Framework Conditions at the Ottawa Conference on Electronic Commerce. These Conditions establish several principles for the good management of consumption taxes on electronic commerce (see Chapter 1 above).

Nevertheless, the impact of the evolution of international commerce in services and intangibles demands a broader reflection beyond the questions raised by e-commerce. The interaction between consumption tax systems operated by individual countries has come under greater scrutiny as potential for double and unintentional non-taxation has increased.

Consumption taxes depend on businesses being responsible for the proper collection and remittance of the revenue. In order to ensure good compliance standards these responsibilities should be as simple, straightforward and certain as possible. To this end administrators need to be aware that complex compliance burdens or unclear rules imposed on business may well result in reduced compliance standards.

Therefore, the Committee on Fiscal Affairs approved in 2003 the creation of the *Consumption Tax Guidance Series* as a means of developing greater awareness of both policy and administrative issues. The initial papers are based on the Committee's work on electronic commerce. Future papers in the Series will flow from the Committee's continuing work programme for consumption taxes. This currently includes taxation of international services and a number of administrative issues.

The Committee on Fiscal Affairs has approved the contents of the Series and countries are encouragecd to apply the guidance wherever possible. Nothing contained in them binds member countries, although where there is clear consensus amongst the member countries, administrations should consider the guidance in the light of their existing taxation systems and their legislative approaches.

Available Papers in the Consumption Tax Guidance Series are annexed in Section II heareafter:

Document 1. Electronic Commerce – Commentary on Place of Consumption for Business to Business Supplies (Business Presence).

Document 2. Electronic Commerce – Simplified Registration Guidance.

Document 3. Verification of Customer Status and Jurisdiction.

In addition there are also administrative issues connected with the growth in international trade which revenue administrations increasingly need to consider and take appropriate actions. Guidance Series in this area are available on *www.oecd.org/ctp/taxguidanceseries.*

I. Consumption Taxation of Cross-border Services and Intangible Property in the Context of E-commerce

A. Guidelines on the definition of the place of consumption

Introduction

1. In 1998, OECD Ministers welcomed a number of Taxation Framework Conditions relating to the consumption taxation of electronic commerce in a cross-border trade environment, including:

i) In order to prevent double taxation, or unintentional non-taxation, rules for the consumption taxation of cross-border trade should result in taxation in the jurisdiction where consumption takes place.

ii) For the purpose of consumption taxes, the supply of digitised products should not be treated as a supply of goods.

iii) Where businesses acquire services and intangible property from a non-resident vendor, consideration should be given to the use of reverse charge, self-assessment or other equivalent mechanism.

2. The Guidelines below are intended to achieve the practical application of the Taxation Framework Conditions in order to prevent double taxation or unintentional non-taxation, particularly in the context of international cross-border electronic commerce. member countries are encouraged to review existing national legislation to determine its compatibility with these Guidelines and to consider any legislative changes necessary to align such legislation with the objectives of the Guidelines. At the same time, member countries should consider any control and enforcement measures necessary for their implementation.

Business-to-business transactions

3. The place of consumption for cross-border supplies of services and intangible property that are capable of delivery from a remote location made to a non-resident business recipient[1] should be the jurisdiction in which the recipient has located its business presence.[2]

4. In certain circumstances, countries may, however, use a different criterion to determine the actual place of consumption, where the application of the approach in paragraph 3 would lead to a distortion of competition or avoidance of tax.[3]

1. This will normally include a "taxable person" or an entity who is registered or is obliged to register and account for tax. This may also include another entity that is identified for tax purposes.
2. The "business presence" is, in principle, the establishment (for example, headquarters, registered office, or a branch of the business) of the recipient to which the supply is made.
3. Such an approach should normally be applied only in the context of a reverse charge or self-assessment mechanism.

Business-to-private consumer transactions

5. The place of consumption for cross-border supplies of services and intangible property that are capable of delivery from a remote location made to a non-resident private recipient[1] should be the jurisdiction in which the recipient has their usual residence.[2]

Application[3]

6. In the context of value-added or other general consumption tax systems, these Guidelines are intended to define the place of consumption (and so the place of taxation) for the international cross-border supply of services and intangible property by non-resident vendors/suppliers that are not otherwise registered and are not required to register in the destination jurisdiction under existing mechanisms.[4, 5]

7. These Guidelines apply to the cross-border supply of services and intangible property, particularly in the context of international cross-border electronic commerce, that are capable of delivery from a remote location.

8. The Guidelines do *not*, therefore, apply to services which are not capable of direct delivery from a remote location (for example, hotel accommodation, transportation or vehicle rental). Nor are they applicable in circumstances where the place of consumption may be readily ascertained, as is the case where a service is performed in the physical presence of both the service provider and the customer (for example, hairdressing), or when the place of consumption can more appropriately be determined by reference to a particular criterion (for example, services related to particular immovable property or goods). Finally, it is recognised that specific types of services, for example, some telecommunications services, may require more specific approaches to determine their place of consumption.[6]

B. Recommended approaches to the practical application of the guidelines on the definition of the place of consumption

Introduction

1. Three tax collection mechanisms are typically used in consumption tax systems: registration, reverse charge/self-assessment, and collection of tax by customs authorities on importation of tangible goods. Under a registration system, the vendor of goods and

1. In other words, a "non-taxable person" or an entity not registered and **not** obliged to register and account for tax.
2. It is recognised that implementing this Guideline will not always result in taxation in the actual place of consumption. Under a "pure" place of consumption test, intangible services are consumed in the place where the customer actually uses the services. However, the mobility of communications is such that to apply a pure place of consumption test would lead to a significant compliance burden for vendors.
3. In accordance with the Ottawa Taxation Framework Conditions, specific measures adopted in relation to the place of taxation by a group of countries that is bound by a common legal framework for their consumption tax systems may, of course, apply to transactions between those countries.
4. While these Guidelines are not intended to apply to sub-national value-added and general consumption taxes, attention should be given to the issues presented, in the international context, relating to these taxes.
5. The objective is to ensure certainty and simplicity for businesses and tax administrations, as well as neutrality via equivalent tax implications for the same products in the same market (*i.e.* avoiding competitive distortions through unintentional non-taxation).
6. When such specific approaches are used, the Working Party recognises the need for further work and for international co-ordination of such arrangements to avoid double or unintentional non-taxation.

services registers with the tax authority and, depending on the design of the tax, either is liable to pay the tax due on the transaction to the tax authority, or collects the tax payable by the customer and remits it to the tax authority. Under the reverse charge/self-assessment system, the customer pays the tax directly to the tax authority. The third approach, collection of the tax on the importation of tangible goods by customs authorities, is common to virtually all national consumption tax systems where national borders exist for customs purposes.

2. Since registration and self-assessment/reverse charge mechanisms are currently in use in the majority of consumption tax systems, they represent a logical starting point in determining which approaches are most appropriate to apply in the context of electronic commerce transactions involving cross-border supplies of services and intangible property.

3. While emerging technology promises to assist in developing innovative approaches to tax collection, and the global nature of electronic commerce suggests that collaborative approaches between revenue authorities will become increasingly important, member countries agree that in the short term, the two traditional approaches to tax collection remain the most promising. However, member countries agree that their application varies depending on the type of transaction.

Recommended approaches

Business-to-business transactions

4. In the context of cross-border business-to-business (B2B) transactions (of the type referred to in the Guidelines), it is recommended that in cases where the supplying business is not registered and is not required to be registered for consumption tax in the country of the recipient business, a self-assessment or reverse charge mechanism should be applied where this type of mechanism is consistent with the overall design of the national consumption tax system.

5. In the context of B2B cross-border transactions in services and intangible property the self-assessment/reverse charge mechanism has a number of key advantages. Firstly, it can be made effective since the tax authority in the country of consumption can verify and enforce compliance. Secondly, given that it applies to the customer, the compliance burden on the vendor or provider of the service or intangible product is minimal. Finally, it reduces the revenue risks associated with the collection of tax by non-resident vendors whether or not that vendor's customers are entitled to deduct the tax or recover it through input tax credits.

6. Member countries may also wish to consider dispensing with the requirement to self-assess or reverse charge the tax in circumstances where the customer would be entitled to fully recover it through deduction or input tax credit.

Business-to-consumer transactions

7. Effective tax collection in respect of business-to-consumer (B2C) cross-border transactions of services and intangible property presents particular challenges. Member countries recognise that no single option, of those examined as part of the international debate, is without significant difficulties. In the medium term, technology-based options offer much potential to support new methods of tax collection. Member countries are expressly committed to further detailed examination of this potential to agree on how it can best be supported and developed.

8. In the interim, where countries consider it necessary, for example because of the potential for distortion of competition or significant present or future revenue loss, a registration system (where consistent with the overall design of the national consumption tax system) should be considered to ensure the collection of tax on B2C transactions.

9. Where countries feel it appropriate to put into effect a registration system in respect of non-resident vendors of services and intangible property not currently registered and not required to be registered for that country's tax, it is recommended that a number of considerations be taken into account. Firstly, consistent with the effective and efficient collection of tax, countries should ensure that the potential compliance burden is minimised. For example, countries may wish to consider registration regimes that include simplified registration requirements for non-resident suppliers (including electronic registration and declaration procedures), possibly combined with limitations on the recovery of input tax in order to reduce risks to the tax authority. Secondly, countries should seek to apply registration thresholds in a non-discriminatory manner. Finally, member countries should consider appropriate control and enforcement measures to ensure compliance, and recognise, in this context, the need for enhanced international administrative co-operation.

II. Consumption Tax Guidance Series
Centre for Tax Policy and Administration

Document 1. Commentary on place of consumption for business-to-business supplies (business presence)

Caveat

Consumption Tax Guidance is a means of developing greater awareness of both policy and administrative issues. On policy issues the Guidance contains recommendations to member governments that are aimed at removing conflicts, distortions and disincentives to international trade. The section on administrative issues has been developed as a result of sharing experiences between member countries. The OECD's Committee on Fiscal Affairs has approved the contents and countries are encouraged to apply the guidance wherever possible. Nothing contained herein binds member countries, although where there is clear consensus amongst the member countries, administrations should consider the guidance in the light of their existing taxation systems and their legislative approaches.

1. A key principle at the basis of the Ottawa Taxation Framework Conditions for consumption taxes is that the rules for the consumption taxation of cross-border electronic commerce should result in taxation in the jurisdiction where consumption takes place.

2. *The Guideline on the Definition of the Place of Consumption for the Taxation of Cross Border Services and Intangible Property in the Context of E-commerce* (the Guideline on the Definition of the Place of Consumption) provides two guidelines for business to business e-commerce transactions for determining the place of consumption for cross-border supplies of services and intangible property made to non-resident business recipients. These two guidelines are referred to in this guidance paper as a "main criterion" and an "override criterion".

3. The main criterion states that the place of consumption for cross-border supplies of services and intangible property that are capable of delivery from a remote location made to a non-resident business recipient should be the jurisdiction in which the recipient has located its business presence.[1]

4. As the main criterion can be considered to be a "proxy" for a pure consumption test (*i.e.* one that approximates where actual consumption occurs), in certain circumstances, countries may use a different criterion to determine the actual place of consumption where the application of the main criterion would lead to a distortion of competition or avoidance of tax,[2] *e.g.* resulting from the routing of services through establishments in non-tax or low-tax jurisdictions. This is referred to as the "override criterion".

5. The Guideline on the Definition of the Place of Consumption clarifies the application of the Guidelines as follows:[3]

a) In the context of value-added or other general consumption tax systems, the Guidelines are intended to define the place of consumption (and so the place of taxation) for the international cross-border supply of services and intangible property.

b) The Guidelines apply to the cross-border supply of services and intangible property, particularly in the context of international cross-border electronic commerce that are capable of delivery from a remote location.

c) The Guidelines do not apply to services which are not capable of direct delivery from a remote location (for example, hotel accommodation, transportation or vehicle rental). Nor are they applicable in circumstances where the place of consumption may be readily ascertained, as is the case where a service is performed in the physical presence of both the service provider and the customer (for example, hairdressing), or when the place of consumption can more appropriately be determined by reference to a particular criterion (for example, services related to particular immovable property or goods).

1. Paragraph 3 of the Guideline on the Definition of the Place of Consumption.
2. Paragraph 4 of the Guideline on the Definition of the Place of Consumption.
3. Paragraph 6, 7 and 8 of the Guideline on the Definition of the Place of Consumption.

Finally, it is recognised that specific types of services, for example, some telecommunications services, may require more specific approaches to determine their place of consumption.

6. The focus of this guidance is to provide commentary building on, but not changing, the Guidelines in the Guideline on the Definition of the Place of Consumption, particularly in instances where the customer has multiple locations.

Application of the main criterion

7. The Guideline on the Definition of the Place of Consumption notes in footnote 2 that the business presence is in principle the establishment of the recipient to which the supply is made.

8. Both business and government members of the Consumption Tax TAG have underlined the importance of contracts in determining the business presence to which the supply is made. By looking at contracts, taxing authorities, suppliers and customers would be able to evidence transactions and justify the treatment given to supplies. Looking at normal commercial practices would appear to be a reasonable approach, as generally, VAT/GST administrations rely on normal commercial practices which are evidenced in the contracts (*e.g.* invoicing, terms of payment, use of intellectual property rights).

Application of the override criterion

9. As noted in the Guideline on the Definition of the Place of Consumption, in certain circumstances, countries may use a different criterion to determine the actual place of consumption, where the application of the approach under the main criterion would lead to distortion of competition or avoidance of tax. In work leading up to the Guideline on the Definition of the Place of Consumption the application of a pure consumption test was examined and it was concluded that this would be burdensome for both business and revenue administrations. However, in cases where competitive distortions or tax avoidance may arise applying the pure consumption test is the only real alternative. Such application may be made, for example, where one or more consuming entities are not entitled to recover the input tax on a transaction that is routed through an associated business presence in a no or low-tax jurisdiction, thus avoiding a significant amount of tax.

10. Where a country invokes the override criterion, it may choose to require a business presence in its jurisdiction to account for tax only to the extent of consumption taking place in that jurisdiction.

11. Where a country invokes the override criterion the host country of the business presence that is considered to have received the supply under the main criterion, may choose to provide a partial credit of its tax which it collected under the main criterion. This credit would be equivalent to that portion of the host country's tax that is attributable to the consumption that is being taxed by the country invoking the override rule. Tax administrations involved in the application of the override criterion should strive to avoid unintentional non-taxation or double taxation.

12. To illustrate, consider a business situated in country A that has contracted for a supply worth $1 000 with 30% of the supply being consumed in country B. The rate of tax is 10% in country A and 20% in country B. In this case country A would require the business to reverse charge on the full value of the supply ($1 000 × 10% or $100). If country B invokes

the override criterion, it would collect \$60 (\$1 000 × 30% × 20%). Country A may subsequently provide a credit of \$30, which is equivalent to that portion of country A's tax collected under the main criterion which is attributable to the consumption being taxed by country B (\$1 000 × 30% × 10%). The net result is that country A and B each tax the value of the consumption that is occurring in their jurisdictions – \$70 in country A and \$60 in country B.

Conclusion

13. The Guidelines on the Definition of the Place of Consumption do not apply to services which are not capable of direct delivery from a remote location or where the place of consumption may be readily ascertained.

14. Where the main criterion is applied, the place of consumption of cross-border electronically delivered services and intangible property is the jurisdiction in which the recipient's business presence is located. Normal commercial practices as evidenced in the terms of the contract (*e.g.* invoicing, terms of payment, use of intellectual property) should normally provide sufficient indicative evidence to assist both business and revenue administrations in determining the jurisdiction of consumption.

15. Countries may use a pure consumption test to determine the place of consumption where the application of the approach under the main criterion would lead to distortion of competition or avoidance of tax. Where a country invokes this approach, it may choose to require a business presence in its jurisdiction to account for tax only to the extent that consumption takes place in that jurisdiction. Where a country invokes this test the host country of the business presence that is considered to have received the supply under the main criterion, may choose to provide a partial credit of its tax which it collected under the main criterion. This credit would be equivalent to that portion of the host country's tax that is attributable to the consumption that is being taxed by the country invoking the override rule.

Document 2. Simplified registration guidance

Caveat

Consumption Tax Guidance is a means of developing greater awareness of both policy and administrative issues. On policy issues the Guidance contains recommendations to member governments that are aimed at removing conflicts, distortions and disincentives to international trade. The section on administrative issues has been developed as a result of sharing experiences between member countries. The OECD's Committee on Fiscal Affairs has approved the contents and countries are encouraged to apply the guidance wherever possible. Nothing contained herein binds member countries, although where there is clear consensus amongst the member countries, administrations should consider the guidance in the light of their existing taxation systems and their legislative approaches.

Introduction

1. Digitally delivered forms of trading provide increased opportunities for vendors in that time and distance are no longer considered barriers. A vendor can make multiple supplies simultaneously in different countries, without developing a physical establishment or presence in any jurisdiction other than his own. As a result, vendors may increasingly find themselves with consumption tax responsibilities in countries in which they have no physical presence and books and records are not maintained.

2. The *Recommended Approaches to the Practical Application of the Guidelines on the Definition of the Place of Consumption* acknowledge that effective tax collection in respect of e-commerce B2C cross border transactions presents particular challenges and that no single option is without difficulties. In the interim they suggest that a simplified registration system be used for the collection of tax on supplies made by non-resident vendors of services and intangible property on B2C transactions where consistent with the overall design of the national consumption tax system.

3. This guidance explores registration and declaration procedures and record-keeping requirements only in the context of simplified registration systems for e-commerce B2C cross border transactions.

Registration procedures

4. Simple registration procedures can be an important incentive to non-resident vendors to begin to engage with the tax authority of a jurisdiction where they may have no link other than the provision of on-line supplies to private customers within the particular jurisdiction.

5. From a vendor's point of view, the simplest way to engage with tax authorities from a remote location is most likely by electronic procedures. A consistent approach to this by tax administrations would further ease the compliance burdens and would have the merit of familiarity for the vendor.

Electronic access to registration application

6. Registration applications could be made accessible on the home page of the tax administration's Web site, preferably available in the languages of the jurisdiction's major trading partners.

Standardisation of registration application

7. The electronic registration application displayed on the Web site could have a standardised layout. The information requested would also be standardised and limited to necessary details such as:

- Name of business (legal and/or trading name).
- Name of contact person responsible for dealing with tax administrations.

- Postal and/or registered address of the business and its contact person.
- Telephone number of contact person.
- Electronic address of contact person.
- Web sites URL of business.
- National tax identification number, if any.

Electronic confirmation of registration

8. The tax administration might undertake to transmit to the vendor confirmation of receipt of the application by electronic means. This would include notifying the vendor of its registration identification number.

Declaration procedures

Electronic filing of declarations

9. Many tax authorities have introduced or are introducing options to submit tax returns electronically. For non-resident vendors required to collect and remit tax to authorities in jurisdictions outside their own, providing the option to file electronically will be essential to facilitating compliance.

Simplified return

10. At the same time, the returns that such vendors will be required to submit should be simple, with minimum data required. Tax authorities could consider a simplified return for non-resident business, which would be less detailed than returns required for local businesses which are entitled to input tax credits.

Standardisation of filing requirements

11. The lack of international consistency in filing requirements, such as reporting periods, forms a drawback for e-commerce vendors. As requirements differ widely between countries, having to file tax returns in a number of countries is a complex process that may impact negatively on the growth of cross-border e-commerce.

12. It is suggested that the information required under international filing requirements, strike a balance between the business need for simplicity and the need for tax administrations to verify whether tax obligations have been correctly fulfilled. Guidance might also be given on the date and frequency for filing tax returns.

Record keeping

13. Tax authorities must be able to review data as a means of assurance that consumption tax has been charged and accounted for in a correct way. In a traditional environment this document is usually paper based. The administrative processes of e-commerce businesses are becoming more and more automated. In the process from ordering, invoicing, and payment the role of paper documents is increasingly being replaced by documents in an electronic format. Non-resident e-commerce vendors, that do not have a physical presence within a jurisdiction, are most unlikely to maintain books and records within the particular jurisdiction.

Electronic records

14. Requirements relating to the use of electronic documents differ widely, as countries may:

- Prohibit the use of electronic documents.
- Require the storage of paper copies of documents.
- Require the use of different formats for official VAT/GST invoices.
- Set specific language requirements.
- Prescribe a specific sequence of invoicing numbers in the country of registration.

15. Where businesses are not allowed to maintain electronic records in accordance with the legislative framework of a jurisdiction, this may be considered to be a barrier. Jurisdictions should be encouraged to review the legal basis for the storage of records and where necessary develop a legal basis to allow for the use of electronic record keeping systems.

Record keeping requirements

16. Businesses that are operating cross-border may be confronted with a multitude of different record keeping requirements in various countries. The formulation of consistent record keeping requirements that might be promulgated and applied internationally is an important instrument to promote voluntary compliance of e-commerce vendors. The development of consistent guidance for the use of electronic records may allow for cost savings by business as well as tax administrations.

17. Standards for the retention of records could be based on what is generally accepted in commercial practice. Revenue authorities' objectives could where possible take into account the existing administrative processes used by businesses.

Summary of conclusions

18. The *Recommended Approaches to the Practical Application of the Guidelines on the Definition of the Place of Consumption* suggest that where a jurisdiction considered it necessary to address consumption tax collection for e-commerce B2C supplies of services and intangible property that consideration be given to implementing a simplified registration system. **These conclusions are made in the context of simplified registration systems for e-commerce B2C cross-border transactions.**

Registration procedures for simplified registration systems

- *Tax administrations are encouraged to provide access to registration applications on their respective Web sites.*
- *Tax administrations are encouraged to develop standardised registration applications requiring minimum details.*
- *Tax administrations are encouraged to confirm the receipt of a registration application and provide the registrant's identification number by electronic means.*

Declaration procedures for non-residents registered under a simplified registration system

- *Tax administrations are encouraged to make available an electronic return template on their respective Web sites.*

- *Tax administrations are encouraged to develop a simplified tax return.*
- *Governments are encouraged to standardise filing requirements.*

Record keeping for non-residents registered under a simplified registration system

- *Tax administrations are encouraged to review the legal basis for the storage of records and where necessary to develop a legal basis to allow for the use of electronic record keeping systems.*
- *Tax administrations are encouraged to base the standards for the retention of records on what is generally accepted commercial practice.*

Document 3. Verification of customer status and jurisdiction

Caveat

Consumption Tax Guidance is a means of developing greater awareness of both policy and administrative issues. On policy issues the Guidance contains recommendations to member governments that are aimed at removing conflicts, distortions and disincentives to international trade. The section on administrative issues has been developed as a result of sharing experiences between member countries. The OECD's Committee on Fiscal Affairs has approved the contents and countries are encouraged to apply the guidance wherever possible. Nothing contained herein binds member countries, although where there is clear consensus amongst the member countries, administrations should consider the guidance in the light of their existing taxation systems and their legislative approaches.

1. A key principle of the Ottawa Taxation Framework Conditions is that the rules for the consumption taxation of cross border electronic commerce should result in taxation in the jurisdiction where consumption takes place.

2. The Guidelines on the Definition of the Place of Consumption for the Consumption Taxation of Cross Border Services and Intangible Property in the Context of E-Commerce provide that the place of consumption, and therefore the place of taxation, for cross border supplies of services and intangible property that are capable of delivery from a remote location, should be the jurisdiction:

i) In which the recipient has located its business presence for business-to-business transactions[1] (B2B); and

ii) In which the recipient has his or her usual place of residence for business-to-consumer transactions (B2C).

3. The recommended collection mechanism for B2B transactions, where the supplying business is not registered and is not required to be registered for consumption tax in the country of the recipient business, is the reverse charge (or self-assessment) mechanism. This means that a supplier would not be required to charge and collect consumption tax on supplies it made to businesses outside its jurisdiction. For B2C transactions the reverse charge/self assessment mechanism was not considered appropriate and in the interim it is acknowledged that where countries consider it necessary, a registration system is currently the only practical means to ensure the collection of tax on B2C transactions. Such a system would require the vendor to collect tax on cross border transactions.

4. The ascertainment of a customer's status (business or private) and jurisdiction is central to the vendor making the right tax decision. The right tax decision depends on whether the customer is established in the same taxing jurisdiction or abroad and whether that customer is a business or a private customer.

5. This guidance paper provides practical guidance on mechanisms that may be used to establish the status (business or private) and jurisdiction of the customer in the context of electronic commerce.

Context

6. The guidance proposed in this paper represents the minimum requirements primarily applicable to low value transactions where the vendor does not have an established relationship with the customer. It does not apply to high value B2B transactions where the vendor and the customer have an established relationship. In these cases the supplier is normally aware of the customer's status and jurisdiction and no additional verification

1. In certain circumstances, countries may use a different criterion to determine the actual place of consumption where the application of the main criterion would lead to a distortion of competition or avoidance of tax. For further information see CTG 003 Commentary on Place of Consumption for Business-to-Business Supplies (Business Presence).

process of the customer's declaration should be necessary. Ultimately the administrative guidance established will need to reflect the realities of the law and practice within a particular jurisdiction.

7. The mechanisms highlighted in this guidance should be considered as a basis for governments to provide clear, realistic and consistent guidance for business on the nature and type of verification that is required to determine the status and jurisdiction of a customer with the expectation that they would follow such guidance in good faith. Revenue authorities should consider the nature, type, scale and quantum of revenue applicable to each transaction when developing guidance, to ensure that the administrative response is weighed against the costs of compliance for business and the revenue at risk.

8. The guidance is designed to be used in cases where taxpayers are attempting to comply with their legal obligations. Nothing in the guidance is designed to limit a country's response to deliberate fraud or evasion.

Conclusion

As the ascertainment of a customer's status (business or private) and jurisdiction is central to the vendor making the right tax decision, revenue authorities should provide guidance to business on the nature and type of verification that is required to determine the status and jurisdiction of a customer. In developing this guidance revenue authorities should consider the nature, type, scale and quantum of revenue applicable to each transaction, to ensure that the administrative response is weighed against the costs of compliance for business and the revenue at risk.

Establishing and verifying the status and jurisdiction of a business customer

9. For low value transactions, where the vendor does not have an established relationship with the customer, the customer's declaration is an essential part of the tax decision process. However, because the reverse charge/self assessment tax collection mechanism[1]

allows business customers to receive the services without being charged tax by the vendor, private customers may have a financial incentive to declare that they are businesses. As a result, customer declarations, when used as the only means of determining the tax jurisdiction, would not be fully reliable.

10. Therefore, in addition to the customer declaration, consideration has been given to three possible methods of verifying the customer declaration

A. Verification of registration numbers.

B. Other indicia.

C. Digital certificates.

1. The reverse charge/self assessment tax collection mechanism is the recommended approach for the collection of tax on B2B supplies.

A) Verification of registration numbers[1]

Online verification

11. Today, at least in some jurisdictions, verifying the status of the customer is a relevant consideration for a vendor in making a taxing decision. For example, within the European Union (EU) the status of the customer in cross border transactions is a significant factor. Supplies to taxable persons who are registered for VAT purposes are subject to a reverse charge/self assessment mechanism, whereas supplies to persons who are not registered for VAT purposes are taxed according to the particular rules that apply to that transaction.

12. In those jurisdictions where the VAT registration status of the customer is significant there appear to be mechanisms to support the decision making process of the vendor. In the case of the EU, the VAT Information Exchange System (VIES) fulfils this role by an online verification system. Other jurisdictions may have similar systems whereby it is possible to check the VAT registration number for validity, albeit not in an automated fashion or in real time.

13. At present, in intra-EU supplies, the customer, if VAT registered, will supply their VAT number to the vendor during the transaction. The customer is making a self-declaration about their status. Where it becomes necessary for the vendor to check the VAT number provided, they can do this by reference to the VIES. The VAT number supplied by the customer can also be used to compare business name and address information contained on the VIES database with name and address information provided by the customer to the vendor.[2]

14. For such an approach to have global application, jurisdictions outside the EU would also need to have a VAT/GST registration database, which is not always the case. Further, the relevant parts of the VAT registration databases of all jurisdictions would need to be publicly available, at least to the extent required to verify individual numbers. This would allow a vendor from any jurisdiction to validate the VAT registration status of a customer from any jurisdiction.

15. As online customers may expect everything to be approved at the time of the transaction, if the VIES or a comparable system is going to be a mandatory part of any transaction there will be very compelling arguments to make online registration data available in a format or interface that allows automated integration with vendors' systems.

16. Because this online method of determining the status of the customer will not always be available a validity computation on declared registration numbers could be used as an alternative.

1. It should be borne in mind that not all jurisdictions use VAT registration numbers and what follows in this section is, therefore, applicable only to those transactions to countries utilising registration numbers.
2. The information may be provided during the transaction or it may be provided as part of some earlier customer registration process and stored in the customer database of the vendor. The vendor may obtain immediate confirmation of the VAT numbers validity of their trading partners through the VIES Web site (accessible by the general public via the Internet) (*http://europa.eu.int/vies*). Nevertheless, traders, making an enquiry as to whether a specific VAT number is correctly associated with a specified trader name and/or address, should go through their national Central Liaison Office which will give one of the following replies: Yes, valid VAT number/No, invalid VAT number/Yes, the VAT number is associated with a given name/address/No, the VAT number is not associated with a given name/address (N.B.: For security and data protection reasons, the national administrations will not supply the name and address in relation to a valid number.)

Computation system

17. This alternative method for online verification of registration numbers would be a validity computation on declared registration numbers, which would only yield a certain answer if the numbers were genuine. This may be an extension of the check digit technique, which is already used for some registration number systems. The diversity of registration numbers, some of which may include alphabetical characters and not all of which will be in the roman character set, means that this process may be quite complex and would therefore not be a short-term solution. In addition, this system may not take into account possible changes in a taxpayer's situation, for example when a taxpayer ceases to be registered in a jurisdiction. The requirement for frequent changes in VAT/registration numbers should also be avoided if this approach is to have merit. Any computation system will need to guard against reverse engineering.

18. Finally, whatever the registration number verification used (online or computation) some private customers may use existing genuine VAT numbers belonging to others to obtain tax-free supplies. Thus, other mechanisms such as indicia and digital certificates should be considered to verify customer's declarations about their status.

B) Indicia

Payment system data

19. A possible method of verifying the status of a customer could be via the payment mechanism. For example, if the customer paid by credit card would it be possible to use card information to determine the status of the customer?

20. Based on the available evidence, it is unlikely that credit card information would in the short term be of assistance in determining the status of a customer. Only minimal information about cardholders is passed to vendors (for privacy protection) and the status of the cardholder is not computable from the card number in the current credit card system.

21. It should be noted that there are commercial reasons to reduce credit card fraud by improving the ability to identify authorised users of the credit card payment facilities. In time these developments may assist in the improved identification of the jurisdiction of a customer.

22. Payment mechanisms such as bank transfer (more used for large-scale transactions than credit cards) and payment arrangements in the contracts may be used as complementary verification methods.

Nature of the supply

23. The nature of the supply may provide an indication of the customer's status. For example, supplies of digitised music or films, with no entitlement to the embedded intellectual property rights, might be indicative that the customer was not VAT registered. Even if the customer is VAT registered it is likely that the supply would be for personal use and not a business input. Using this same indicative approach, business accounting software is much more likely to be a B2B rather than a B2C sale.

24. Even if the nature of the supply can offer reasonable presumptions there are limitations to this method of verifying the status of the customer. For example, it could be

difficult to distinguish between anti-virus software sold to a private customer and the same software sold to a small business for business purposes.

C) Digital certificates

25. The use of digital certificates may help determine the tax status of a customer. Some jurisdictions have issued digital certificates for business-to-government (B2G) transactions and some companies are issuing digital certificates to their customers. Tax authorities should normally be able to recognize the authenticity of digital certificates where they are interoperable (such as being based on the x.509 standard) and are issued in a high integrity manner.

26. The integrity of such certificates includes consideration about who issued the certificate, how the information contained on the certificate was validated and whether there is scope to include particular information about VAT registration status and jurisdiction. If these matters could be addressed this approach offers the best possibilities, because it could be conducted in real-time and with greater reliability than other methods.

Mismatch of customer self declaration with other indicia

27. In cases where the customer's self declaration is not in agreement with other indicia used to verify the declaration, revenue authorities should consider providing additional domestic guidance as to how to tax these transactions. Where the vendor cannot regard the customer as a business customer, because, for example, the customer cannot provide a valid VAT number or digital certificate, this might lead to the presumption that it is a private customer and VAT should be charged accordingly.

Conclusions

For low-value transactions, where a vendor and customer do not have an established trading relationship, some of the criteria above may be used to verify the declaration of the customer.

The jurisdiction of the business customer should be ascertained in the same way, and at the same time as its status. For example, online verification of the VAT number may allow verification of the jurisdiction of the customer (in or outside the jurisdiction of the vendor) and their VAT registration status at the same moment, where the VAT registration number contains a country code, or some similar device.

Revenue authorities should consider providing additional domestic guidance as to how to tax a transaction, where the self-declaration of the customer is not in agreement with other indicia used.

Where the vendor cannot regard the customer as a business customer, because, for example, the customer cannot provide a valid VAT number or digital certificate, this might lead to the presumption that it is a private customer and VAT should be charged accordingly.

Establishing the jurisdiction of a private customer

28. In order to make the right tax decision for a supply to a private customer, a vendor must determine the jurisdiction of the customer. Verification of the private customer

jurisdiction cannot be grounded in a single and simple mechanism such as an identification number. This means that revenue authorities should be encouraged to provide more certainty through clear public guidance.

Declaration of the customer

29. It is clear that customer self-declaration, when used as the only means of determining the jurisdiction would have limited reliability. The obvious limitation is that the customer can change their declaration to achieve the outcome that they desire if it is not possible to independently confirm the information provided. In some jurisdictions a false declaration by a customer may be an offence under the laws of the country. If this is the case it is recommended that business provide appropriate warnings to customers to this effect. Nevertheless, information provided by the customer (jurisdiction and detailed address) may be regarded as an important element to determine jurisdiction in association with a range of other criteria consistent with business practice and the importance of the transaction.

Payment information

30. A possible method of determining the status or jurisdiction of a customer could be via the payment mechanism. For example, if the customer paid by credit card would it be possible to use card information to identify the customer's jurisdiction?

31. Based on current evidence it is unlikely that credit card information will always be of assistance in determining the jurisdiction of a customer in the short term. Nevertheless, the development of new security technologies and payment systems should be kept under review. Other payments methods – *e.g.*, by bank transfer – may supply useful confirmatory data.

32. Where confirmation of the billing address is requested as part of the commercial processing of an on-line transaction, it would however be reasonable to expect a very high level of correlation with the customers declared taxing jurisdiction.

Tracking/Geolocation software

33. Geolocation technologies use various information sources to determine the location of an Internet user based on the user's Internet Protocol (IP) address. In recent court cases Internet experts have claimed that technologies achieved 85% accuracy.

34. To determine jurisdiction from an IP number, the destination IP number is compared to a database of geographically known IP numbers. Varying degrees of accuracy (up to 96%) are claimed for such systems, which are increasingly being used by Internet businesses for targeting advertising and for some fraud control purposes. IP number tracing is readily available in many common computer operating systems and in inexpensive software for most common computer platforms.

35. The advantage of technology-based verification is that it is likely to be easily and relatively cheaply incorporated into online transactions.

36. Clarification or agreement between the relevant revenue authority and the business sector as to what rules should be applied in the scenario where an instance of a customer's self declaration of jurisdiction does not match the jurisdiction indicated by a verification technology or system is desirable. The solution should seek to strike an appropriate balance between the genuine concerns of business regarding lost sales, their need for tax certainty and the need for protection of the consumption tax revenue base by governments.

Nature of the supply

37. Another possible source of evidence to ascertain the jurisdiction of the customer can be based on the features of the supply. A combination of features including language, content and currency may assist in providing indications of the intended destination of a supply.

Digital certificates

38. From a technical point of view, digital certificates offer the best possibilities in the long term, but the use of digital certificates is even less widespread among private customers than among businesses. Consequently, this should only be considered as a long-term solution.

Conclusions

Taking into account the prevailing technologies, the recommended approach at this time is to obtain a customer declaration with the full address of usual place of residence substantiated by other indicia or verification tools, according to the nature, type, scale and quantum of the transaction.

Information provided by the customer (jurisdiction and detailed address) may be regarded as an important element to determine jurisdiction in association with a range of other criteria. Other criteria that may be used by a vendor to substantiate the declaration of the customer include payment information, tracking/geolocation software, nature of the supply, and digital certificates.

Revenue authorities should consider providing additional domestic guidance as to how to tax a transaction where a customer's self declaration of jurisdiction does not match the jurisdiction indicated by other indicia.

Periodic review

39. The technology that supports e-commerce can change very quickly. Any method used to determine the status and jurisdiction of a customer may rapidly be superseded by developments. Therefore it is suggested that this issue be kept under periodic review.

40. One development that should be monitored is the Universal User Profile whereby a user's passwords and other identity information are stored with a service provider to facilitate easy access to a range of Web sites and services. Microsoft.NET Passport, AOL's Magic Carpet and the Liberty Alliance are examples of these developments. "Verified by Visa" and "MasterCard's SPA" initiatives also provide merchants with tools to verify customer identity. These effectively replace the real world signature with a password. While it is unclear whether these solutions could provide jurisdictional information, further monitoring of Universal User Profile solutions, should be undertaken.

41. By following the suggestions contained in this paper, revenue authorities and businesses will establish a framework in which there is an explicit, but not onerous, process to obtain information from the customer for the vendor to make a reasonable tax decision, consistent with any other data used obtained for commercial or other purposes.

42. The actual details of how the information is obtained, by question and answer, provision of digital certificate or other means is a variable element which sits inside the framework and which can be adjusted to keep pace with technology.

43. In considering changes to the information it is suggested that revenue authorities always seek to move closer to a 100% accurate answer to the questions of status and jurisdiction and that they use means which are, wherever possible, in common commercial practice or which are otherwise not onerous for businesses to adopt.

Summary of conclusions – Recommended approaches

44. It should be noted that these conclusions refer to low-value transactions where the vendor does not have an established relationship with the customer. The guidance should be seen as minimum requirements in the absence of better information or solutions available to the vendor.

Recommended approaches to overall verification issues

- Revenue authorities should provide guidance to business on the nature and type of verification that is required to determine the status and jurisdiction of a customer.
- Revenue authorities should consider the nature, type, scale and quantum of revenue applicable to each transaction when developing guidance, to ensure that the administrative response is weighed against the costs of compliance for business and the revenue at risk.

Recommended approaches to establishing and verifying the status and jurisdiction of the business customer

- Where a vendor and customer do not have an established trading relationship, a customer declaration, supported by criteria such as on-line verification of registration numbers, computation systems, payment system data, nature of the supply, and digital certificates may be used to confirm that the customer is registered for consumption tax in their country of origin.
- The jurisdiction of the business customer should be ascertained in the same way, at the same time as its status. When the customer is proved to be an entity with a valid foreign VAT number, this should be accepted as verification of jurisdiction.
- It is suggested that revenue authorities consider providing additional domestic guidance as to how to tax a transaction where a customer's self-declaration of jurisdiction does not match the jurisdiction indicated by other indicia.
- Where the vendor cannot regard the customer as a business customer, for reasons such as the customer not providing a valid VAT number or digital certificate, or absence of other supporting indicia, this might lead to the presumption that it is a private customer.

Recommended approaches to establishing the jurisdiction of a private customer

- Information provided by the customer (jurisdiction and detailed address) may be regarded as an important element to determine jurisdiction in association with a range of other criteria.
- Other criteria that may be used by a vendor to substantiate the declaration of the customer include payment information, tracking/geolocation software, nature of the supply, and digital certificates.

- It is suggested that revenue authorities consider providing additional domestic guidance as to how to tax a transaction where a customer's self-declaration of jurisdiction does not match the jurisdiction indicated by other indicia.

Periodic review

- Revenue authorities are encouraged to continue to monitor technology and business developments that may assist in the determination of customer jurisdiction.

ANNEX 3

Environmentally related taxes

The following tables show the structure of revenues from environmentally related taxes for pollution control and related trends. They present revenue raised from different individual tax bases in million USD, its share of GDP and of total tax revenue.

Environmentally-related taxes are defined as any compulsory, unrequited payment to general government (benefits provided by government to taxpayers are not normally in proportion to their payments) levied on tax bases deemed to be of particular environmental relevance.

Pollution-oriented environmentally relevant tax bases include energy products, motor vehicles and transport, waste management, ozone depleting substances and other.

This information is taken from the "*OECD Environmental Data Compendium 2004*". The tables on environmentally related taxes may be consulted free of charge at the following address: *www.oecd.org/env/tax-database*.

Structure of revenues from environmentally related taxes,[1] 1995, 2001

1995

Tax bases	CAN	MEX	USA	JPN	KOR	AUS	NZL	AUT	BEL	CZE	DNK	FIN	FRA	DEU	GRC	HUN	ISL
Energy products	7 803	2 700	55 253	53 615	4 816	7 729	650	3 133	4 346	1 389	3 859	2 727	31 011	49 505	3 282	1 194	95
For transport purposes	*7 803*	*2 700*	*35 517#*	*44 557*	*4 816*	*7 729*	*650*									*1 189*	*95*
Petrol			20 228	28 992	0	0					1 335						95
Diesel			6 940		0	0	0										0
For stationary purposes		*0*	*0*	*9 058*	*0*	*0*	*0*									*5*	*0*
Fossil fuels		0	0	5 454	0	0	0									5	0
Electricity		0	0	3 604	0	0	0			0				4 243		0	0
Motor vehicles and transport	2 030	584	23 487	35 605	6 251	2 288	369	2 475	1 698	183	3 576	1 008	4 342	9 629	1 428	53	102
One-off import or sales taxes	2	104		6 496	3 778		0		0	0	2 657	615	0	0	725	0	38
Recurrent taxes on registration or road use	1 531	480		29 109	2 473		369		1 698	183	919	393	4 238	9 629	703	53	63
Other transport taxes	497	0	5 519	0	0	0	0	0	0	0	0	0	104	0	0	0	0
Waste management		0	390	0	0		0	28	0	42	268	28	3 313	0	0	0	5
Final disposal		0	0	0	0		0	28	0	42	110	0	3 223	0	0		0
Packaging		0	0	0	0		0	0	0	0	85	24	90	0	0		5
Other waste-related product taxes		0	390	0	0		0	0	0	0	72	5	0	0	0		0
Ozone-depleting substances	69	0	616	0	0	0	0	0	0	2	0	0	0	0	0	0	0
Other	0	0	2 073	32	0	0	0	28	0	84	170	3	76	32	0	52	0
Total	9 903	3 283	81 819	89 252	11 067	10 017	1 019	5 664	6 045	1 700	7 874	3 766	38 742	59 166	4 709	1 299	202
% of GDP	1.7	1.1	1.1	1.7	2.3	2.8	1.7	2.4	2.2	3.3	4.4	2.9	2.5	2.4	4.0	2.9	3.0
% of tax revenue	4.7	6.9	4.1	6.0	11.0	9.1	4.5	5.8	4.9	8.2	8.8	6.5	5.7	6.3	12.7	6.9	9.3

1. Data refer to revenues from environmentally related taxes for pollution control, in million USD at current prices and exchange rates.

Structure of revenues from environmentally related taxes,[1] 1995, 2001 *(cont.)*

1995

Tax bases	IRL	ITA	LUX	NLD	NOR	POL	PRT	SVK	ESP	SWE	CHE	TUR	UKD	Total[2]	% of total/ % du total
Energy products	1 152	36 066	576	6 770	3 289	1 675	2 909	396	10 321	5 557	3 614	3 387	26 170	334 989	71.9
For transport purposes													*23 855*	128 910	27.7
Petrol										2 382			15 763	68 796	14.8
Diesel													8 092	15 032	3.2
For stationary purposes													*2 315*	11 378	2.4
Fossil fuels														5 459	1.2
Electricity		3 716	7		696				0	904				13 170	2.8
Motor vehicles and transport	861	3 977	28	5 704	1 817	252	997	46	2 309	834	2 574	718	6 775	121 998	26.2
One-off import or sales taxes	463		0	2 577	1 196		881	0	972	246	0	527	0	21 276	4.6
Recurrent taxes on registration or road use	397		28	3 127	555		116	46	1 337	568	2 574	191	6 240	67 019	14.4
Other transport taxes	0	0	0	0	66		0	0	0	21	0	0	535	6 743	1.4
Waste management	0	0	0	125	16	0	0	0	0	0	0	0	0	4 217	0.9
Final disposal	0	0	0	125	0	0	0	0	0	0	0	0	0	3 529	0.8
Packaging/emballage	0	0	0	0	16	0	0	0	0	0	0	0	0	220	0.0
Other waste-related product taxes	0	0	0	0	0	0	0	0	0	0	0	0	0	467	0.1
Ozone-depleting substances	0	0	0	0	0	0	0	0	0	0	0	0	0	687	0.1
Other	0	0	0	1 235	63	0	10	0	0	43	27	0	0	3 928	0.8
Total	2 013	40 043	604	13 834	5 186	1 926	3 916	442	12 630	6 434	6 215	4 105	32 945	465 819	100.0
% of GDP/% du PIB	3.0	3.6	3.3	3.3	3.5	1.5	3.7	2.3	2.2	2.6	2.0	2.4	2.9	2.0	. .
% of tax revenue	9.2	8.9	7.9	8.0	8.5	3.8	11.1	. .	6.6	5.6	6.0	10.7	8.3	6.4	. .

1. Data refer to revenues from environmentally related taxes for pollution control, in million USD at current prices and exchange rates.
2. Percentages data exclude Slovak Republic.

Structure of revenues from environmentally related taxes,[1] 1995, 2001 (*cont.*)

2001

Tax bases	CAN	MEX	USA	JPN	KOR	AUS	NZL	AUT	BEL	CZE	DNK	FIN	FRA	DEU	GRC	HUN	ISL
Energy products	7 588	9 227	64 734	43 430	10 672	6 264	492	3 246	3 271	1 404	4 207	2 415	22 565	40 190	2 034	1 271	76
For transport purposes	*7 588*	*9 227*	*39 766*	*36 510*	*10 672*	*6 264*	*492*									*1 209*	*76*
Petrol			20 868	25 632	0	3 612					1 220						76
Diesel			8 209		0	2 651	0										0
For stationary purposes		*0*	*0*	*6 920*	*0*	*0*	*0*									*62*	*0*
Fossil fuels		0	0	3 884	0	0	0									10	0
Electricity		0	0	3 036	0	0	0			17				3 860		52	0
Motor vehicles and transport	1 817	1 605	29 158	28 709	3 873	859	321	2 329	1 876	185	2 718	1 212	3 157	7 479	922	92	106
One-off import or sales taxes	4	493		3 703	2 250		0		0	0	1 485	823	0	0	0	0	29
Recurrent taxes on registration or road use	1 813	1 111		25 006	1 623		321		1 876	185	1 169	388	3 156	7 479	922	92	77
Other transport taxes	0	0	8 521	0	0	0	0	0	0	0	64	0	1	0	0	0	0
Waste management		0	355	0	0		0	79	2	46	263	42	3 063	0	0	0	7
Final disposal		0	0	0	0		0	79	0	46	128	28	3 063	0	0		0
Packaging		0	0	0	0		0	0	0	0	71	12		0	0		6
Other waste-related product taxes		0	355	0	0		0	0	2	0	64	3	0	0	0		2
Ozone-depleting substances	97	0	32	0	0	0	0	0	0	1	5	0	0	0	0	0	0
Other	0	0	1 138	25	0	0	0	34	0	39	292	2	477	21	0	48	0
Total	9 502	10 832	95 417	72 163	14 545	7 122	813	5 688	5 148	1 676	7 486	3 671	29 261	47 690	2 956	1 412	190
% of GDP/% du PIB	1.3	1.7	0.9	1.7	3.4	2.0	1.6	3.0	2.3	2.9	4.7	3.0	2.2	2.6	2.5	2.7	2.5
% of tax revenue/% du total des recettes fiscales	3.8	9.3	3.3	6.4	12.5	6.4	4.6	6.6	5.0	7.6	9.4	6.6	4.9	7.0	6.9	7.0	6.8

1. Data refer to revenues from environmentally related taxes for pollution control, in million USD at current prices and exchange rates.

Structure of revenues from environmentally related taxes,[1] 1995, 2001 (cont.)

2001

Tax bases	IRL	ITA	LUX	NLD	NOR	POL	PRT	SVK	ESP	SWE	CHE	TUR	UKD	Total[2]	% of total/ % du total
Energy products	1 227	260 806	541	7 331	2 920	3 336	1 954	376	8 841	5 316	2 901	4 617	32 967	322 218	72.3
For transport purposes													*3 1951*	143 754	32.3
Petrol										2334			18 877	72 619	16.3
Diesel													12 774	23 634	5.3
For stationary purposes													*1 016*	7 998	1.8
Fossil fuels														3 894	0.9
Electricity		2 181	5		683				587	1 374				11 95	2.6
Motor vehicles and transport	1 183	5 041	25	5 269	1 913	105	1 271	45	2 137	679	2 407	901	7 080	11 4473	25.7
One-off import or sales taxes	704		0	2 621	1121		1 095	0	1 075	0	202	425	0	16 030	3.6
Recurrent taxes on registration or road use	479		25	2 648	633		177	45	1 062	679	2 205	476	5 886	59 534	13.4
Other transport taxes	0	0	0	0	159		0	0	0	0	0	0	1 194	9 939	2.2
Waste managementts	0	0	0	165	113	0	0	0	0	91	17	0	732	4 976	1.1
Final disposal	0	0	0	165	53	0	0	0	0	91	17	0	732	4 402	1.0
Packaging/emballage	0	0	0	0	61	0	0	0	0	0	0	0	0	149	0.0
Other waste-related product taxes	0	0	0	0	0	0	0	0	0	0	0	0	0	424	0.1
Ozone-depleting substances	0	0	0	0	0	0	0	0	0	0	0	0	0	135	0.0
Other	0	0	0	1 234	41	0	1	0	0	59	73	0	294	3 779	0.8
Total	2 410	31 847	566	13 999	4 987	3 441	3 226	421	10 978	6 146	5 399	5 518	41 072	445 582	100.0
% of GDP	2.4	2.9	2.9	3.7	2.9	1.9	2.9	2.1	1.9	2.8	2.2	3.8	2.9	1.8	. .
% of tax revenue	7.9	7.0	7.0	9.2	6.8	5.8	8.8	6.4	5.4	5.4	7.2	10.4	7.7	5.8	. .

1. Date refer to revenues from environmentally related taxes for pollution control, in million USD at current prices andexchange rates.
2. Percentages data exclude Slovak Republic.

Trends in revenues from environmentally related taxes,[1] 1995-2001 *(cont.)*

	% of GDP							% of tax revenue						
	1995	1996	1997	1998	1999	2000	2001	1995	1996	1997	1998	1999	2000	2001
Canada	1.7	1.7	1.6	1.6	1.5	1.4	1.3	4.7	4.6	4.4	4.3	4.1	3.8	3.8
Mexico	1.1	1.0	1.3	1.8	2.1	1.4	1.7	6.9	5.9	7.4	11.1	12.4	7.8	9.3
USA	1.1	1.0	1.0	1.0	1.0	1.0	0.9	4.1	3.6	3.6	3.6	3.6	3.4	3.3
Japan	1.7	1.7	1.7	1.7	1.7	1.7	1.7	6.0	6.1	5.9	6.3	6.5	6.2	6.4
Korea	2.3	2.6	2.8	2.8	2.9	3.1	3.4	11.0	12.1	12.3	12.3	12.4	11.7	12.5
Australia	2.8	2.7	3.0	2.6	2.5	2.1	2.0	9.1	8.6	9.6	8.2	7.9	6.5	6.4
New Zealand	1.7	1.7	1.7	1.8	1.7	1.6	1.6	4.5	4.7	4.7	5.1	4.9	4.7	4.6
Austria	2.4	2.7	2.7	2.7	2.7	2.8	3.0	5.8	6.1	6.2	6.0	6.1	6.4	6.6
Belgium	2.2	2.5	2.5	2.4	2.4	2.3	2.3	4.9	5.5	5.4	5.3	5.2	5.0	5.0
Czech Republic	3.3	3.0	2.9	2.9	3.0	2.9	2.9	8.2	7.7	7.5	7.5	7.8	7.3	7.6
Denmark	4.4	4.6	4.7	5.1	5.2	4.8	4.7	8.8	9.2	9.3	10.2	10.1	9.8	9.4
Finland	2.9	3.2	3.3	3.4	3.5	3.2	3.0	6.5	6.8	7.1	7.4	7.4	6.7	6.6
France	2.5	2.5	2.4	2.5	2.6	2.4	2.2	5.7	5.6	5.3	5.6	5.6	5.3	4.9
Germany	2.4	2.3	2.2	2.2	2.3	2.4	2.6	6.3	6.1	5.9	5.8	6.1	6.3	7.0
Greece	4.0	4.1	3.9	3.6	3.1	2.7	2.5	12.7	12.8	11.7	10.0	8.4	7.2	6.9
Hungary	2.9	2.9	2.9	3.3	3.2	2.9	2.7	6.9	7.0	7.5	8.6	8.2	7.4	7.0
Iceland	3.0	3.1	3.1	3.2	3.3	3.1	2.5	9.3	9.4	9.6	9.1	8.9	8.1	6.8
Ireland	3.0	3.1	3.0	2.9	2.9	2.9	2.4	9.2	9.3	9.2	9.3	9.5	9.3	7.9
Italy	3.6	3.5	3.5	3.3	3.3	3.0	..	8.9	8.3	8.0	7.8	7.7	7.2	..
Luxembourg	3.3	3.3	3.1	3.0	3.0	2.9	2.9	7.9	7.7	7.6	7.5	7.4	7.1	7.0
Netherlands	3.3	3.6	3.6	3.5	3.8	3.7	3.7	8.0	8.7	8.6	8.8	9.1	9.0	9.2
Norway	3.5	3.7	3.6	3.5	3.3	2.9	2.9	8.5	9.1	8.7	8.1	8.1	7.5	6.8
Poland	1.5	1.7	1.6	1.6	1.9	1.9	1.9	3.8	4.2	4.2	4.4	5.5	5.7	5.8
Portugal	3.7	3.7	3.5	3.6	3.6	3.0	2.9	11.1	11.5	10.5	10.9	10.5	8.9	8.8
Slovak Republic	2.3	2.2	2.1	1.9	2.0	2.2	2.1	..	..	..	5.3	5.8	6.2	6.4
Spain	2.2	2.1	2.1	2.2	2.1	2.0	1.9	6.6	6.6	6.4	6.5	6.0	5.6	5.4
Sweden	2.6	3.1	2.9	2.9	2.9	2.8	2.8	5.6	6.4	6.0	5.9	5.4	5.1	5.4
Switzerland	2.0	2.1	2.0	2.1	2.1	2.2	2.2	6.0	6.1	5.8	6.0	7.2	6.9	7.2
Turkey	2.4	3.1	3.1	2.9	3.7	3.7	3.8	10.7	12.4	11.0	10.2	11.7	11.0	10.4
UK	2.9	2.9	2.9	3.2	3.2	3.1	2.9	8.3	8.4	8.4	8.6	8.9	8.3	7.7
North America	1.1	1.0	1.1	1.1	1.1	1.0	1.0	4.2	3.8	3.8	3.9	3.9	3.5	3.6
OECD Europe	2.7	2.8	2.7	2.8	2.8	2.7	2.7	7.0	7.0	6.9	7.0	7.1	6.8	6.7
EU	2.8	2.8	2.8	2.8	2.8	2.7	2.7	7.0	7.0	6.9	6.9	7.0	6.7	6.7
OECD	1.9	1.9	1.9	1.9	1.9	1.8	1.8	6.1	6.0	5.8	5.8	5.9	5.5	5.5

1. Date refer to revenues from environmentally related taxes for pollution control, in million USD at current prices and exchange rates.
2. Percentages data exclude Slovak Republic.

OECD PUBLICATIONS, 2, rue André-Pascal, 75775 PARIS CEDEX 16
PRINTED IN FRANCE
(23 2005 01 1 P) ISBN 92-64-00676-1 – No. 53873 2005